GW00360068

THE
MALDIVES

WHITE STAR
PUBLISHERS

THE MALDIVES

Written by
Kurt Amsler

Photography by
Kurt Amsler

Biological Files Written by
Angelo Mojetta

Editorial Supervision by
Valeria Manferto De Fabianis
Laura Accomazzo

Translation by
Antony Shugaar

Graphic Supervision by
Patrizia Balocco Lovisetti

The texts concerning the following dives were written by Claudio Cangini:
Helengeli Thila; Felivaru — Shipyard; Kureddu — Express;
Madivaru Kandu; Mulaku Kandu; Vattaru; Rakeedhoo;
Embudhu Kandu

Special thanks go to the diving guides of the various diving centers who provided information and drawings which were invaluable in the preparation of this guide: Peter Christoffersson, Staffan Hanson, Heiri Loetscher, Christina Michael, Tommy Oggenfuss, Tashi Recordati, and Robert Schneider.

The publisher would also like to thank *Seafari Adventures*, of Monza, Italy (Via Francesco Frisi 20; Tel. 39.39.329338) for their kind and generous assistance.

Cover

A closely-packed school of snapper (Lutjanidae sp.).

*Top left
A group of rays (Pygoplites diacanthus).*

Back cover

*Top
Elegant Platax teira (Platax teira).*

*Center
A royal angel fish (Taeniura sp.).*

*Bottom
The route of a dive at Embudhu Kandu, on South Male.*

© 2003 White Star S.r.l.
Via Candido Sassone, 22-24
13100 Vercelli, Italy
www.whitestar.it

All rights reserved. No part of this publication may be reproduced, stored in a retrieval system or transmitted in any form or by any means, electronic, mechanical, photocopying, recording or otherwise, without written permission from the publisher.

ISBN 88-8095-661-2
REPRINTS:
1 2 3 4 5 6   07 06 05 04 03

Printed by C&C Offset Printing Co. LTD, China

Contents

1 Elegant batfish (Platax teira) swim toward the ocean surface.

4-5 This aerial photograph offers a view of the distinctive configuration of the atolls that make up the archipelago of the Maldives.

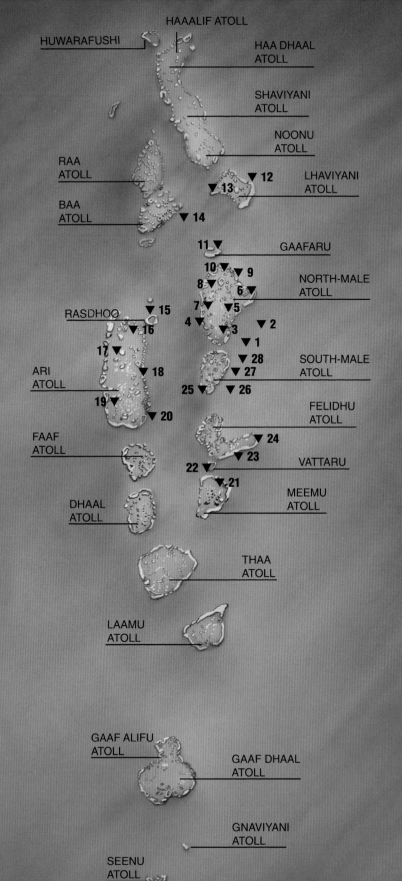

HAAALIF ATOLL

HUWARAFUSHI

HAA DHAAL
ATOLL

SHAVIYANI
ATOLL

NOONU
ATOLL

RAA
ATOLL

▼ 12   LHAVIYANI
▼ 13   ATOLL

BAA
ATOLL

▼ 14

11 ▼   GAAFARU

10 ▼ ▼ 9

8 ▼   ▼ 6   NORTH-MALE
ATOLL

7 ▼   ▼ 5

RASDHOO   ▼ 15

4 ▼ ▼ 3   ▼ 2

▼ 16

▼ 1

17 ▼

▼ 28   SOUTH-MALE
ATOLL

ARI
ATOLL   ▼ 18   ▼ 27

25 ▼   ▼ 26

19 ▼

▼ 20   FELIDHU
ATOLL

FAAF
ATOLL   ▼ 24

▼ 23   VATTARU

22 ▼

▼ 21   MEEMU
ATOLL

DHAAL
ATOLL

THAA
ATOLL

LAAMU
ATOLL

GAAF ALIFU
ATOLL

GAAF DHAAL
ATOLL

GNAVIYANI
ATOLL

SEENU
ATOLL

N

INTRODUCTION

From the airplane, a fabulous panorama stretches out before my eyes. The Maldives, nothing more than so many dots on the endless seascape of the Indian Ocean. Green islands surrounded by vibrant rings of sand extend across an emerald green lagoon, which further out plunges down into the dark blue of the abyss. The "realm of the thousand islands" is a translation of the word "Maldive," of Sanskrit origin. Located about eight hundred kilometers (about five hundred miles) to the southwest of Sri Lanka, these islands stretch in a narrow line of atolls that cuts the equator from 7° 9' north latitude to 0° 45' south latitude, and from 72° 30' until 73° 43' east longitude. The atolls extend seven hundred sixty kilometers (four hundred seventy-five miles) from north to south, and from east to west, one hundred thirty kilometers (eighty miles), a truly vast territory, but with a ridiculously small total land area, of only two hundred ninety-eight square kilometers (one hundred eleven square miles).

A - Sights such as this make a diver's heart race: through the crystal-clear water of the lagoon, one can clearly see the base of the barrier reef, and the point at which it drops away into the deep.

B - These reefs, which are created through the tireless work of billions of tiny polyps, develop into sinuous shapes, at times breaking the ocean's surface.

There are more than one thousand islands, subdivided among nineteen atolls, that form this country; only two hundred of these islands, however, are inhabited.

At the center of the archipelago lies the island of Male, with the capital city of the same name, which is indeed the only true city in the Maldives. The vegetation is truly luxuriant on all of the islands. Lakes and streams are uncommon, inasmuch as these islands are made up of coral limestone.

In geological terms, the Maldives are the summit of a submarine mountain chain, which begins three hundred or four hundred kilometers (one hundred ninety to two hundred fifty miles) west of India, and then extends over two thousand three hundred kilometers (1,435 miles) to the south. This underwater mountain chain rises from depths of four thousand meters up to shallows of only seventy meters (two hundred thirty feet) beneath the surface. This ridge serves as the foundation for the reefs that owe their existence to a type of small animal, the coral polyp. The polyps, only a few millimeters in size, live in enormous colonies, separated one from another only by small limestone cells. When they die, their descendents take up residence upon the old skeletons, and begin to build new little cells. In general terms, this is how - first - a coral formation develops, and later, an entire reef. The coral polyps feed on the plankton that they take from the water. The rate of growth of a branch or of a coral reef depends upon the abundance of plankton, on currents, and on other factors. These coral formations take on the widest variety of appearances.

The Maldives are considered to be a classic region of atolls, including the largest ones that can be found on the planet. The Maldives are one of the most coral-rich regions in the world. There are over seventy species here, especially acropora, which take first place as reef-builders. These same reefs, along with their excellent location in the Indian Ocean, are responsible for the enormous wealth and variety of the marine life forms of the archipelago.

A

B

DIVING IN THE MALDIVES

Diving in the Maldives is organized in the most exemplary of fashions. Every tourist facility possesses a base of some sort for divers and, depending on the size of the island, of one or two boats at the divers' disposal. The bases are generally equipped to provide services for divers who are already certified and experienced.

They also offer courses for beginners. A great deal of success has crowned the programs for advanced instruction for experienced divers.

Participants in these teaching initiatives are introduced to a number of special techniques and a great variety of scuba activities, among which we should make particular note of:
- night-time diving;
- ecological navigation;
- marine biology;
- drift diving;
- diving into wrecks;
- photography and video.

Taking a diving cruise is certainly the best way to experience the allure of this marvelous archipelago, since it also allows one to explore the most unspoiled seabeds, which cannot be reached from the tourist villages.

The boats used on these tours are comfortable wooden motoryachts of at least twenty meters (about sixty-five feet) in length, with well-ventilated double cabins, toilets with showers, and plenty of living room. This hotel-boat, capable of accommodating no more than ten passengers, is followed by a support boat which — equipped with a compressor, tanks, and weights — makes it possible to do scuba diving in the safest and easiest way. In the Maldives, there are three categories of dives:
- the dives done inside the atolls;
- the dives done outside the atolls;
- the dives done inside the channels, or passes.

In this same order are generally classified the different levels of skill. The diving sites that are described in this book cover all categories and every level of difficulty. Just as the diving sites are differentiated, we can categorize the techniques that must be adopted.

C

C - This picture seems to be an image out of a dream: magically set upon enchanting crystal-clear waters, a small and verdant island fringed with palm trees breaks the line of the horizon.

D - It is absolutely impossible to calculate the exact number of atolls that make up the archipelago of the

D

Maldives; in fact, aside from the major atolls, there are also many islets covered only by scattered shrubs and short strips of sand, which may be swept away during the course of a tropical storm.

E - Beginning just a few inches beneath the ocean surface, one can already see the incredible richness and variety of life forms of the seabeds. In the distance, one can recognize the island of Ihuru, in the atoll of North-Male.

E

Therefore, we shall have:
- diving from the shore
- diving from a moored boat
- drift diving.

The Maldives are a region that is perfectly suited for drift diving. For a number of years now, therefore, the foundations have been laid for diving with an ecological awareness, and they call for this technique, particularly useful in preventing the destruction of the coral reefs themselves through constant anchoring. Drift-diving, especially at first, can prove to be somewhat demanding for the scuba divers, or force them to make some changes in their usual techniques. All the same, this type of diving is far more enjoyable and rewarding. Prerequisites for successful drift diving are a good briefing, meaning a careful and thorough discussion of the dive to be made, and an expert and well trained crew on board the boat. Slowly, but with growing popularity, the parachute is being used, and is doing a great deal for diver safety. This signal buoy that forms part of the team's equipment can be allowed to bob to the surface during the safety stop. In this way, the crew of the boat can see the position of the scuba team as they make their way along the reef, even from a considerable distance, and bring the boat to within hailing distance. Especially when the ocean is rough, or when the crew is looking for divers against the light, the bright colors of the buoy floating high above the waves can be seen far better than the dark heads of divers. Leaving aside this type of accessory equipment, in the Maldives regular modern diving equipment is standard. It includes:
- buoyancy compensator;
- chronometers;
- a octopus;
- depth indicators.

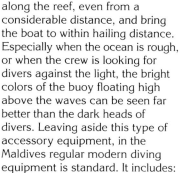

A

B
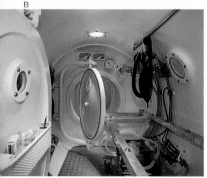

A - Travelling from island to island aboard a comfortable boat is without a doubt the best way to tour the archipelago of the Maldives. This picture shows one of the cruise ships of the Seafari Adventures Viaggi of Monza, Italy), which allow one to reach diving sites far away from the tourist villages.

B - On the island of Bandos, a thoroughly modern decompression chamber has been installed, capable of accomodating four persons.

C - A number of scuba divers make a safety stop with their "parachutes," giving the crew of the boat time to sight them and safely recover them.

D - Two scuba divers prepare to explore a wreck that lies on the sandy seabed of the waters around the island of Hembadhu.

C

D

The use of the "padi-wheel" or of a modern underwater computer is extremely advisable, inasmuch as the topography of the ocean bed is far from homogeneous, and calls for what is known as "multilevel diving." Moreover, with these helpful modern instruments, one can far better enjoy one's down-time, as it were. One rule that applies everywhere in the Maldives prohibits dives that go beyond the down-time, thus making safety stops necessary. This regulation is more than reasonable.

Emergency transportation from the more distant atolls or from the safari-routes all the way to the modern, professional, and reliable decompression chambers on the island of Bandos is possible.

The water temperature tends to be well above twenty degrees centigrade throughout the entire year. As a thermal protection, all one needs is a simple 3-millimeter neoprene wetsuit.

For scuba divers who are less sensitive to the cold, a wetsuit, made of padded, insulated nylon is sufficient.

As one has clearly had a chance to realize, in this divers' paradise called the Maldives, it is the rule for all divers to pay adequate respect to environmental considerations and to safety requirements.

All of this has been made possible by a far-sighted government and through the prudence and sense of responsibility of those who run the diving bases. The underlying philosophy of this book respects these same principles and is meant to encourage them in their work. In the description given of each diving site, there is further specific information in the headings of "Respect for the Environment" and "Safety".

LET SCUBA DIVERS BE THE GUARDIANS OF THE UNDERWATER ENVIRONMENT

We scuba divers are only visiting strangers in the underwater world, and we should always be well aware that this delicate structure, this array of life cycles, can be damaged — perhaps irreparably — by the slightest of missteps. Nowadays, it is inconceivable that a scuba diver should intentionally damage the underwater world or knowingly undermine the survival of any of its rightful inhabitants. Nevertheless, a great deal of harm can be done through ignorance and a lack of understanding about ocean life forms.

THE CORAL REEF

Made up of billions of minuscule animals - the so-called coral polyps - a coral reef constitutes the abode and the staff of life for all forms of ocean life. Corals are fragile structures, which break at the slightest impact. In order to dive with the proper care for the environment, therefore, one must distribute one's weights perfectly. One should take particular care while taking underwater photographs or shooting underwater footage. While, composing a shot, one tends to pay less attention to surrounding objects. Just a contact of a finger or glove with the surface of the coral, whether that is a hard or a soft coral, can wound and even kill the tiny creatures - polyps - that make up coral. If one cannot avoid leaning against or holding the coral, one should do so only at fingertip touch.

FEEDING THE ANIMALS IN THE OCEAN

Feeding the animals in the ocean - the fish, chiefly - is certainly fun to do. It tends to be an essentially one-sided bargain, and therefore a bad idea. In areas where people have been feeding the fish for years, behavioral deformations have been observed that are quite sobering. Groupers and moray eels that were once quite inoffensive have become voracious predators. In these areas, it has become not uncommon for fish to attack scuba divers, causing some serious bite-wounds. Moreover, in the majority of cases, the food that is given to these fish is radically different from their normal diet. As a result of fish-feeding, some very large humphead wrasses died after being fed dozens of eggs, while a great many soldierfish choked to death after wolfing down chicken bones. Large basses have been seen to tear little sacks of food right out of the scuba diver's hand, devouring both sack and contents. The consequences of having such indigestible foreign bodies in the fish's digestive tract can be easily imagined. If the final objective is to get close enough to these fish to observe them closely, one need not rely upon food to do so. Rather, one should simply study the behavior of the various life forms, one should dive calmly and carefully, with the correct distribution of ballast, one should breathe very slowly and move painstakingly toward the creature in question, a little bit at a time.

One will soon find that in this way it is possible to observe, photograph, and film every creature in one's immediate surroundings.

PLAYING WITH THE FISH

Seizing and holding underwater animals is unfortunately a fairly common habit. Certainly, the chief unfortunate butt of this behavior is the pufferfish. When this fish feels threatened, it protects itself from its enemies by inflating itself with water, though it thus makes it impossible for the fish to flee. For the fish, however, this state of emergency inflation causes enormous physical strain to the entire body. Marine biologists have determined that after a total number of inflations ranging from ten to fifteen, the pufferfish will die. Most fish, moreover, have a

E, F, G - Alcyonarians, acropora, and large gorgonians are distinctive features of the reefs of the Maldives, offering a delicate alternation of shapes and hues.

H - Blackspotted stingrays (Taeniura melanospilos) are found throughout the Indian Ocean. They live by preference on sandy seabeds or in shallow lagoons. They generally show no fear of humans, indeed, they often seek out physical contact with scuba divers.

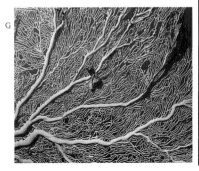

very fine layer of mucous on their skin or on their scales, which serves to prevent the invasion of parasites. Even if one takes the greatest possible care, this protection can be damaged by anyone stroking or seizing the fish. Undesired guests tend to settle in immediately, and while these new parasites may not be life-threatening to the fish, they definitely cause pain and discomfort and can damage the fish's health. One can also cause impact lesions on the animal's internal organs by trying to drag them out of their hiding places, or by moving mollusks, or shell fish into a better position for photography.

SOUVENIRS

Both in ocean waters and other waters there are extremely complex and sophisticated life cycles in which every building block fits directly atop another. If a single component part should be lacking, then the operation of this structure of life cycles begins to falter and may even break down entirely. Of course, the consequences are a function of the number of building blocks that are removed. Until attaining a certain critical mass of insults and attacks, Nature is able to absorb and regenerate. Innumberable instances, however, show us far too clearly that the reserves are not inexhaustible! Sea shells are often brought back from holidays as souvenirs and are therefore much sought after. All the various types of seashell, however, play important roles. Some kind of seashells battle other forms of life that - were they to proliferate - endanger the ecosystem. One obligatory example is the the great triton. This is the only natural enemy of the crown of thorns (Acanthaster placi), a predatory starfish that can gobble up as much as six square meters (sixty-five square feet) of coral surface in just a month's time. The tritons are quite in demand as souvenirs, and therefore these animals have undergone wholesale slaughter worldwide. Now that it has been deprived of its natural enemy, the crown of thorns is multiplying at a dizzying rate, which is causing a mass destruction of coral reefs of terrifying proportions. Often dead shells can be found on the reef floor, the victims of the many predators present in the reef. Even these shells should be left where they lie, because in most cases they are occupied by a hermit crab, which must move from residence to residence in order to accommodate its astonishing rate of growth.

Sea turtles belong to one of the most endangered species in the world, and they are protected by international laws. Despite that, in the world every year at least 50,000 of these creatures are slaughtered. Sea turtles lose their lives in order to be transformed into personal accessories of all sorts, turtle soups and steaks, tortoise-shell eyeglass frames and brooches, components of cosmetics, sunning creams, and especially souvenirs. It should be clear to any scuba diver that it is our duty to refuse to purchase articles of this sort. Each individual scuba diver should work to defend these ocean creatures, to help the species survive.

DANGERS AMONG THE FISH AND CORAL AND IN THE ENVIRONMENT

A - This photograph shows us a number of dramatic sequences in the struggle between a triton (Charonia tritonis) and a crown of thorns (Acantasther planci), the sea star that is responsible for the destruction of huge stretches of coral reef.

B - Cypraeae (Cyprea vitellus) only move on the seabed by night; during the day they remain hidden in the sand or amidst the coral.

The waters of the Maldives abound in ocean currents. Both surface and deep-water currents can pose considerable obstacles and even physical dangers to scuba divers. As scuba divers, we should be well aware that wind, waves, and currents are forces of Nature, which we must respect. Therefore, with the knowledge that we possess about them, we must plan our dives and complete our supplies and equipment. For all of the diving sites presented in this book, we provide — under the heading "Safety" — specific information concerning the conditions that prevail, but we must devoutly recommend the specific briefing that only the diving instructor can provide. There is no need to be afraid of the various forms of life, especially of sharks, barracudas, and other large predatory fish. One must fear small and hard-to-spot creatures, often exceedingly well camouflaged. These little menaces rely on massively powerful venoms that are very dangerous to humans. All of these creatures, however, make use of their armament in an exclusively passive manner. The most numerous species found in the Maldives is that of the scorpionfish, which includes, the *Pterois volitans*, the *P. radiata* and the stonefish *(Synanceia verrucosa)*. All three of these species possess sharp spines which are associated with venom glands. If these spines come into contact with the human body, the fish deftly injects a powerful neurotoxin. The consequences are immediate nausea, followed by lancing pains, swelling of the part of the body that has been stung, cardiorespiratory insufficiency, sweating, and fever. It is important to remember that heat can neutralize the neurotoxin. Soak the part of the body that has been stung in very hot water or else place very hot packs upon it. This can reduce the effects of the sting. If the scuba diver behaves correctly, however, touching nothing, not leaning against corals, and not walking on the summit of the reef, then the danger of being stung by a scorpion fish is eliminated. Jellyfish and sea anemones both cause itching, stinging, and swelling, as do a number of the corals that belong to the class *Hydrozoa*, which is to say, yellow fire corals, which have a capsule structure, which allows them to launch thousands of tiny venomous darts. Not all humans react to these venoms in the same manner.

C - The stonefish (Synanceia verrucosa), an authentic master of camouflage, is the most venomous creature of the undersea world. It has, in fact, fourteen dorsal-fin spines that secrete an exceedingly powerful poison, which can be fatal in some cases. The stonefish, however, uses its lethal weapons solely as weapons of self-defense.

D - Swimming with its pectoral fins spread, a clearfin turkeyfish (Pterois radiata) drives its prey — mostly sweepers or Anthias — into a corner from which it is difficult to escape.

E - The red fire coral was first noted in the Maldives in 1983. It is thought that this species migrated here from the Philippines, though it is not clear how the larvae could have survived so long a voyage.

UNDERWATER PHOTOGRAPHY

Given the manifold aspects of the underwater universe of the Maldives and the splendid colors of the fish and the coral, it is almost a moral obligation to pause for a while with a camera before these wonders of nature. With a camera in hand, one tends to observe everything more closely, one learns to understand better the behavior of the undersea creatures, and one just generally experiences the underwater world in a more intense manner. Nowadays there are modern, easy-to-use underwater cameras available on the market that allow one to take high-quality photographs. The most famous are the amphibious cameras, such as *Motormarine* and *Nikonos*. Modern automatic surface cameras can be fitted with specially constructed underwater cases. The waters of the Maldives are particularly well suited for underwater photography. One important prerequisite for good photography is that the water be crystal clear. Of course, even in the Maldives there are days or seasons of the year when the water is less than perfectly transparent, but it is extremely unlikely that it should become impossible to photograph. As a matter of course, an underwater photographer can expect to have ideal conditions here. Natural lighting plays a very important role. It would be a mistake to think that because one is using a flash one need not take daylight into consideration. Especially in wide-angle photography, this is a crucial factor. In the Maldives, the underwater photographer can find the best subjects in the upper layers of water, which is to say from a depth of one to twenty meters (three to sixty-five feet). Here, the sunlight is always strong enough to enchant a photographer, with lovely clear blue backdrops that are highlighted by the light of the flash. These environmental conditions allow the use of films with ordinary speed. The best results can be obtained with 100 ASA. In the waters of the Maldives, Fuji RDP film performs extremely well, and reproduces the finest blues and the liveliest reds. As we have already pointed out, in order to obtain good color in one's photographs, it is necessary to make use of an underwater flash. Since water density tends to filter the spectrum of sunlight, at a distance of three or four meters (ten to twelve feet), even the most garish and spectacular corals and fish would appear only a dull blue-

greenish color on film. For all those who dive without tanks, and who therefore take photographs only in the top five meters (fifteen feet or so) of water, the best photographs can be obtained with special "Underwater Films" from *Kodak*, which are particularly sensitive to red, and which therefore amplify the red spectrum of sunlight underwater. When using this film, of course, one cannot make use of a flash, or the photographs would be too red. The possibilities for the underwater photographer in the Maldives are endless, and therefore constitute an ongoing challenge for the underwater photographer who dives here. Panoramic shots with divers or schools of fish swimming over the reef are always spectacular. Whenever diving into one of the wrecks described in this book, it would be wise to bring a camera with one. For shots of this sort, one should use a wide-angle lens. Of course, the best suited lenses are those with focal lengths between 20 and 14 millimeters. With a lens with a normal focal length, in fact, the photographer would have to move quite far from the subject in order to fit it all into the composition. The rays of light, which are after all the medium through which the picture is finally imprinted upon the film, would in this case be required to make too long a trip through the water, and the photograph would be a dull blueish-green without contrast.

Therefore, in addition to the advantage of close-up photography, these wide-angle or fisheye lenses give the entire photography a considerable sharpness of perspective. For subjects of a smaller size - for photographs of scuba divers and small schools of fish, for example - the ideal focal lengths range from 20 to 28 mm. If the photographer succeeds in holding his camera at a distance of eighty to one hundred fifty centimeters (thirty to sixty inches), then the result will be extremely sharp, high-contrast photographers with extremely lifelike color. For individual fish, anemones with clownfish, views of coral formations, sponges, and gorgonians, the best lenses to use range from 35 to 50 millimeters. With these lenses, the sharpness of focus is not optimal. The photographer must take care

C

A

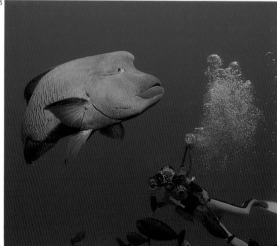
B

A - The photographer shown here is using a Nikonos V with a 15 mm lens. In order to obtain a better distribution of light, he is using two flashes.

B - The large humphead wrasse (Cheilinus undulatus) shows absolutely no fear when confronted with a scuba divers; it is therefore one of the underwater photographer's favorite subjects.

then to select an F-stop of between 8 and 11. This means that the distance from the subject of the shot should be no greater than about a meter (just over three feet), or better yet, even closer. The uncanny world of close-up and macro photography should never be overlooked by any underwater photographer. Nearby, above, and inside the corals live countless animalcules. A number of details of soft coral, anemones, sponges, and many blennies and gobies all belong to the remarkable list of ideal macro subjects.

The technique involved in focusing correctly on these tiny subjects is quite simple. Depending on what camera one is using, one will add lenses, intermediate rings, or specific macro lenses. If one uses them with a TTL flash, one can then be sure that one will automatically have the precise lighting of the picture. In salt water, one should take particular care of underwater photographic equipment. After every dive, the camera should be washed, and even left to soak in a fresh-water bath for ten minutes, because this is the only way of ensuring that all of the particles of sand and the salt crystals can be removed from the joints and from the *O-rings*. In order to make absolutely certain that the camera and the flash are waterproof, one should check the *O-ring* each time one changes film. One can free the *O-ring* from residue and grime by removing it with one's fingers, which will also allow one to check for damage or technical problems. The seating of the *O-ring* (female) should be cleaned with a kleenex. The black Neoprene *O-rings* should be oiled ever so slightly. The orange silicon *O-rings* should be oiled abundantly before they will be truly waterproof. While flying, driving from place to place, and when aboard a *dhoni*, it would be wisest to pack the camera in a small carrying case made of a high-impact synthetic material with a polystyrene covering; we might mention the *Pelicase*, for example. To guard against any mishap, bring a great number of rolls of film, and do not overlook adequate supplies of spare batteries, spare O-rings, and everything you will need for maintenance and minor repairs.

D

C - Modern reflex cameras can also be equipped for underwater use. The photographer shown in this picture is using a Sea & Sea reflex system and a Sea & Sea TTL flash.

D - A group of blotcheye soldierfish (Myripristis murdjan), illuminated by the light of the flash, show the brilliant red of their coloration.

E

E - This scuba diver, intently taking a macro photograph, is using a Motormarine II.

F - After an exciting dive, the camera is readied for new adventures.

F

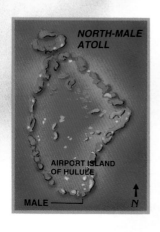

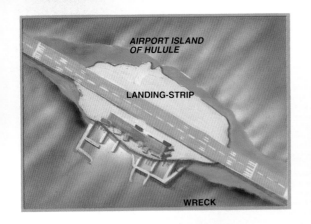

AIRPORT ISLAND
OF HULULE

LANDING-STRIP

WRECK

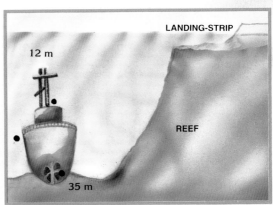

LANDING-STRIP

12 m

REEF

35 m

LOCATION

The wreck of the *Maldive Victory* lies on the western side of the airport-island of Hulule, precisely near the first quarter of the southern side of the landing strip. The wreck lies parallel to the reef, on the sandy seabed at a depth of thirty-five meters (one hundred fifteen feet), upright and with the bowsprit pointing north.

HISTORY

In the early morning hours of 13 February 1981, a Friday, this 35,000-ton freighter ran at full speed onto the southern tip of the airport-island. Since it had not been built with watertight bulkheads, the ship sank in the space of about an hour even though the hole was fairly small. The sailors and the few passengers aboard managed to make their way to the landing strip, only about thirty meters (a hundred feet) away; all were rescued, and none were even injured.
The freighter was only ten years old, and hailed from Singapore; the holds were full of merchandise, chiefly for the tourist facilities. Panic spread through the island when it became known that the long-awaited foodstuffs and building materials were lying on the bottom of the ocean, and so a number of salvage teams quickly assembled, made up mostly of local divers but also by diving instructors from

A, B, C, D - It was Friday, the 13th of February, 1981 when the Maldive Victory, *running at considerable speed, sailed past the port of Male, and smashed into the reef that surrounds the island of Hulule. The freighter sank in the course of a few hours with its entire cargo. We dove down to the wreck just a few hours later, and these photographs document a truly remarkable situation: the structures and the interiors were still so completely intact that one did not at all feel that one was in a wreck.*

A

B

C

D

E - The bow of the Maldive Victory stands out sharply against the surface, a monument to human error and weakness.

F, G - Here the captain of the Maldive Victory once gave orders to the crew, but now nature rules all; everything has undergone a sea-change, now covered with corals.

nearby islands. They were successful in bringing a great deal of merchandise to the shore, but most of the goods had been ruined by contact with the salt water, and the financial loss was enormous. Sea water, which exerted so much pressure at the depth of thirty-five meters (one hundred fifteen feet) that corks were actually pushed back into the the bottles, penetrated into thousands of bottles of wine and other types of liquor. Even two brand-new automobiles, which

had been loaded onto the deck, were turned into useless hulks. Even today, bits of scattered cargo are found in the hold of this 110-meter-long (360-foot-long) wreck.

DIVES

The location of the wreck is marked by a buoy, to which boats can be moored. The powerful currents between Male and Hulule make it absolutely essential to use a line to dive and to return to the surface. Normally, one starts from the mainmast, which rises to a

G - The huge prow of the wreck reaches vainly into the open ocean. The freighter, which had a displacement of 35,000 tons , was one hundred ten meters (three hundred sixty feet) in length. When it sank, it was carrying two brand-new limousines, construction material, foodstuffs, and liquor, mostly destined for the tourist villages.

A, B - The metal
structures of the
freighter, after ten
years underwater,
are already heavily
encrusted with corals
and other mineral
growths, and already
fit right in with the
underwater
seascape.

depth of just twelve meters (about forty feet) beneath the surface of the water. Once one reaches the deck, the superstructures serve as a shelter against the currents. The holds are wide open and one can easily swim into them. In the wheelhouse, there is nothing of any particular interest, since all of the ship's technical fittings and equipment — such as the compass, helm, and even the shipboard telegraph, which was a popular subject for underwater photographers for some ten years' time — have disappeared.

For those exploring the inner bulkheads, which can be reached by swimming down stairways and along wide corridors, we advise bringing a good flashlight and the assistance of a divemaster, unless of course one knows the ship like the back of one's hand.

LIFE FORMS

Even just a few hours after the Maldive Victory sank, a great number of fish had begun to establish residence in and about the ship. For more than a decade now, the superstructures have been patrolled by a large school of batfish *(Platax teira)*, while a number of barracuda *(Sphyraena sp.)* hover above the deck; those who swim around the wreck are provided with an escort of humphead wrasses *(Cheilinus undulatus)*. Large schools of fusiliers *(Caesio sp.)* dart through the water, as a foreshadowing of the fact that in the pipes, passageways, and nooks and crannies of this ship, one will encounter all of the animal species that can normally be found on reefs, and in grottoes and underwater caverns.

During a number of dives, one will encounter a large sea turtle sleeping at the tip of the bowsprit of the *Maldive Victory*.

SAFETY

Dives to the *Maldive Victory* can be classified as advanced dives. The depth of twenty-five meters (eight-two feet) on the deck is no particular problem, but great caution, planning, and experience are required in order to deal with

C - The Maldive
Victory has become
home to a number
of fish, including a
great many pinnate
batfish (Platax
teira), humphead
wrasse (Cheilinus
undulatus),
barracudas
(Sphyraena sp.),
and large schools of
fusiliers (Caesio sp.).

D - Diving down
into a wreck is
always a
remarkably exciting
experience.
The emotional
involvement
increases
considerably if one
knows the story
and events that lay
behind the loss of
the vessel: exploring
the empty decks
and the ghostly
rooms, one sees the
ship come to
ghostly life, and the
many details spring
into a new
perspective.

G

E - Diving down into the Maldive Victory *is recommended only to scuba divers who are quite experienced, not so much because of the depth and the position in which the sunken freighter lies, but because of the powerful currents, which can create considerable difficulties.*

F, H - Nature has taken over the power windlass, whose shape can still be guessed at beneath the coral encrustations.

G - A comparison with a scuba diver allows one to form some idea of the size of the huge screw, which lies on the seabed at a depth of about thirty-five meters, or a hundred feet, constituting the deepest section of the Maldive Victory.

the currents, which can be quite powerful at times. It is crucial to use lines along which to dive and to return to the surface.

The wreck is one hundred ten meters (three hundred sixty feet) in length, but by following the charts offered in this volume, one can plan one's dive in accordance with the air supply and the time available, completing the entire dive in safety and returning to the mooring lines attached to the buoy. It is important to remember that he wreck is studded with extremely sharp jagged seashells and urticating hydroids. Moreover, injuries can be caused by sharp jagged fragments of metal.

RESPECT FOR THE ENVIRONMENT

Although sunken ships are inanimate objects, over the course of the years they are transformed into artificial reefs. On the whole, then, the same rules apply that one would follow on a coral reef: stay a safe distance away from the structures and, when one is making one's way through narrow

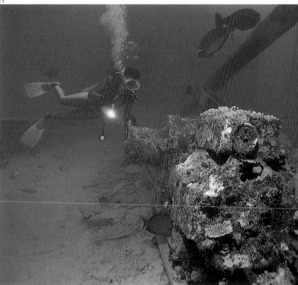

passages, be especially careful not to damage coral formations with one's fins.

On the other hand, in contrast with the situation on coral reefs, one is allowed to wear protective gloves.

PHOTOGRAPHY

In order to fit the largest possible view of the ship into a composition, make use of super-wide-angle lenses, or else fisheye lenses. For narrower shots, or else to take pictures of fish and other creatures, one can use any other focal length.

The mainmast, with scuba divers against the light is a good prop, together with the enormous propellers, of course, which can be compared with the size of a fellow scuba diver.

KUDAHAA - RAINBOW

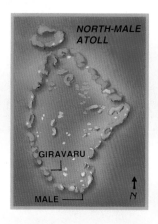

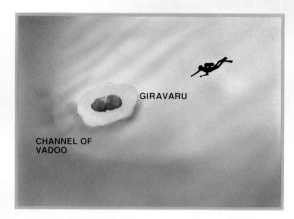

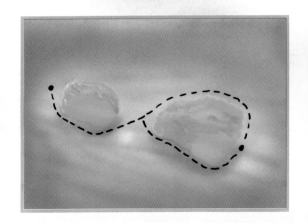

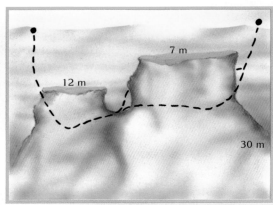

7 m

12 m

30 m

LOCATION

Rainbow lies on the southwest side of the North-Male Atoll, inside the barrier reef. The nearest island is Giravaru. The diving site contains two underwater *thilas* which are some sixty meters (about two hundred feet) apart. Around the two coral tables — which are both circular, and which lie, respectively seven meters (twenty-three feet) and twelve meters (forty feet) beneath the surface of the water — the seabed quickly drops away to a depth of thirty meters (one hundred feet).

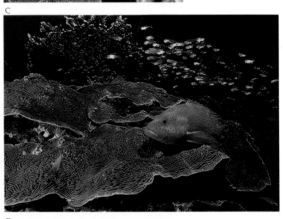

DIVES

On Rainbow, boats should not and need not be moored.
It is uncommon for the currents to be very strong, and therefore it is almost always possible to swim around both *thilas*. Since the top of the reef lies at a depth of seven meters (twenty-three feet), the three minutes of safety stop at a depth of five meters (about sixteen feet) should be done in the open water with a parachute. This diving area is suited to any level of experience.

LIFE FORMS

The underwater world is an authentic kaleidoscope of colors, with as a background a living wall of thousands of *Anthias* (*Pseudanthias squamipinnis*), which swarm amidst the coral masses of the peak and the tough black and green acropora (*Dendrophyllia sp.*) on the sheer reef walls. On the edge of the reef grow enormous coral table, where large nurse sharks

A - A great many morays have established their dens in the grottoes and crannies of the reef. In this picture, one can see a giant moray (Gymnothorax javanicus), one of the most common in the waters off the Maldives.

B - Little scalefin Anthias (Pseudanthias squamipinnis) with their garish orange coloring add even more color to the reef walls.

C - The coral grouper (Cephalopholis miniata) is a daunting predator, that feeds mostly on glassfish and Anthias.

D - Like all the other members of its species, this triggerfish (Balistapus undulatus) also presents a remarkable shape, different from that of other fish. The head measures about a third of the length of the body, and the powerful teeth allow the fish to grind the shells of the mollusks, crabs, and sea urchins on which it feeds.

(Nebrius ferrugineus) can often be found slumbering away. Also on the reef, amidst the large coral blocks, it is possible to see large morays *(Gymnothorax javanicus)*. Around both of the *thila* one also encounters numerous blue triggerfish *(Pseudobalistes fuscus)*, oriented with their heads facing the reef: when scuba divers draw near they dart like lightning into their holes, so that only their tails poke out. Large sea turtles are not uncommon.

RESPECT FOR THE ENVIRONMENT

Special attention should be paid to jutting rock, upon which the tough black and green acropora grow in great numbers.
It is therefore to have the proper buoyancy control and always to maintain a safe distance from the reef itself.
Let us also point out that although the morays *(Gymnothorax sp.)* may often seem to be quite sociable and approachable, one should

always refrain from touching them, as this can only do them harm. The same is true for nurse sharks *(Nebrius ferrugineus)* and sea turtles.

PHOTOGRAPHY

In this location, the photographer can use fisheye lenses up to macro, lenses successfully at any focal length. Suggested composition is the seascape with countless *Anthias (Pseudanthias squamipinnis)*.

E - A large sea fan stands out sharply against the surface of the sea; around it is a wreath of the inevitable Anthias.

F - A small group of bluegreen chromis (Chromis viridis) *meanders over the reef, near an (acropora).*

G -The tentacles of a number of large sea anemones drift in rhytyhm to the flow of the current.

H - The Maldive anemonefish (Amphiprion nigripes) *and the sea anemone offer an excellent example of symbiotic life forms: the anemonefish finds shelter and protection among the tentacles of the sea anemone, whose stings all other species of fish avoid.*

I - A nurse shark (Nebrius ferrugineus) *sleeps on the seabed, in the shelter of two jutting rocks.*

BODU BANANA - BANANA REEF

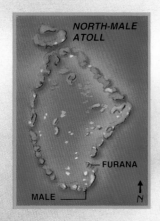

NORTH-MALE ATOLL

FURANA

MALE

N

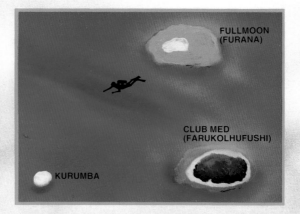

FULLMOON (FURANA)

CLUB MED (FARUKOLHUFUSHI)

KURUMBA

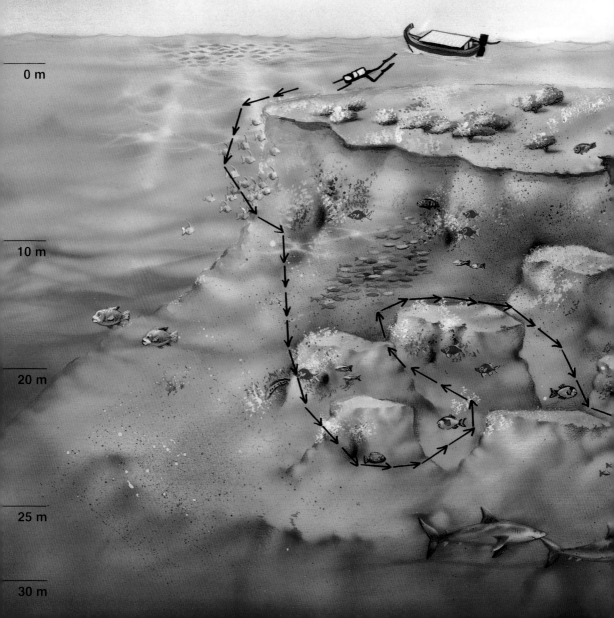

0 m

10 m

20 m

25 m

30 m

BANANA

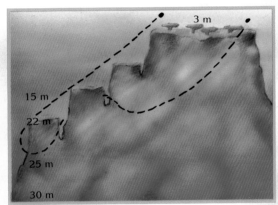

3 m

15 m

22 m

25 m

30 m

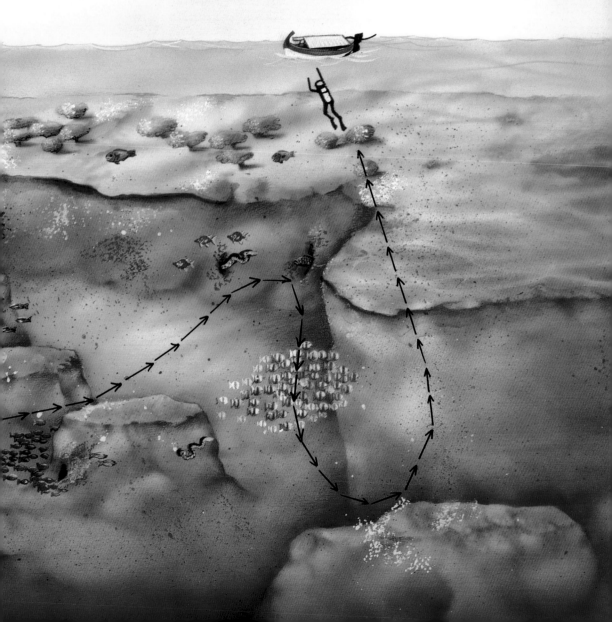

LOCATION

Banana Reef lies on the eastern side of the Male-North Atoll, inside the barrier reef. Nearby islands include Fullmoon Island, Farukolhufushi, and Kurumba. This reef, with its elongated form, which is in fact reminiscent of a banana in shape, stretches from northeast to south over a length of some three hundred meters (about a thousand feet). Ever since scuba divers began to visit this part of the North-Male Atoll, twenty years ago, Banana Reef has remained an ideal spot. As in a great many other places around the Maldives, the divers have caused no adverse effects upon the seascape and, if we may, fishscape. Indeed, it seems that year after year on Banana Reef the fish population simply continues to grow. The upper section of the reef lies at a depth of just three meters (ten feet) beneath the surface of the water, but on the western side the reef plunges to a depth of thirty meters (a hundred feet) and more. The western side is also the best place to dive, since there are seven major coral agglomerations here that form an uncanny seascape.

DIVES

On Banana Reef, only drift dives are possible. The unbelievable abundance of fish and the

presence of many varieties of coral are clearly the result of the virtually incessant currents, which are obviously a major factor in determing the directions of one's dive. It is at any rate possible to halt even in the presence of the strongest currents, by taking shelter in grottoes or in the lee of enormous masses of coral.

LIFE FORMS

The stars of this reef are certainly the five hundred or so bannerfish (Heniochus diphreutes) which tend to concentrate on the northeastern side of Banana Reef. If the currents are right, however, one can sight a number of grey reef sharks (Carcharhinus amblyrhynchos), even without

A - Like many other fish, the coral grouper (Cephalopholis miniata) is plagued by many parasites that infest its skin, its brachial fissures, and its opercula. Tiny cleaning shrimp help to rid the fish of these unwanted guests, using their efficient sharp claws.

B - At Banana Reef it is common to encounter large specimens of the humphead wrasse (Cheilinus undulatus), which grow to be two meters (six-and-a-half feet) in length and to weigh 170 kilograms (375 pounds).

C - This picture shows a giant moray (Gymnothorax javanicus) in its den.

D - Where the currents are powerful and the flow of plankton is rich, conditions are favorable for the development of gorgonians and alcyonarians.

E - A group of saber squirrelfish (Sargocentron spiniferum) takes shelter behind the reef.

F - The younger specimens of the emperor angelfish (Pomacanthus imperator) present a dark-blue coloring with light-colored concentric stripes, which terminate in a closed circle on the caudal peduncle.

making use of bait. Normally, moreover, divers almost always enjoy the company of humphead wrasses (Cheilinus undulatus). Among the enormous masses of coral swim oriental sweetlips (Plectorhyncus orientalis). Large moray eels (Gymnothorax sp.) peek out of their grottoes. Further out to sea, instead, huge numbers of school-dwelling fish swim, foremost among them metallic-blue fusiliers (Caesio lunaris). The soldierfish (Myripristis murdjan), on the other hand, are bright red, and they move in tight formation amongst the underwater cliffs, where groupers can be found measuring up to and more than a meter (about a yard).

SAFETY

Depending on the season, weather conditions, and the tides, Banana Reef may be swept by extremely powerful currents which can, in some cases, be dangerous: the surface of the water actually seems to boil. In the so-called spin-cycle, an inlet on the reef is named the Washing Machine; in that place there are vertical currents that can drag an unwary scuba diver down to a depth of thirty meters (one hundred feet). If this should happen to the reader, the thing to do is remain calm, because there will be a corresponding up-current that will spit the scuba diver out into calmer waters. Since the current tends to drag scuba divers at the end of the dive out to the open water, each team should take along a parachute. It is only in this manner that the crew of the boat can be certain of finding lost divers.

RESPECT FOR THE ENVIRONMENT

The fish in this area show absolutely no timidity in the presence of scuba divers. One should, however, refrain from touching the morays (Gymnothorax sp.) or the humphead wrasses (Cheilinus undulatus) because, as we explained in the first part of this book, one is simply doing our finny friends less than no good at all. And when filming or photographing anything, stay at an appropriate distance from the reef, lest one should damage the corals.

PHOTOGRAPHY

Since the fish show absolutely no fear of photographers on this reef, one can take excellent shots, as long as the currents are running properly. Suggested focal lengths: from 28 to 50 millimeters. In the presence of powerful currents, it is impossible to stand still to take photographs. Nonetheless, no photographer who cares about the environment would seize the coral in order to steady himself, thus damaging the underwater world for the sake of a mere photograph.

A

A - A numerous school of soldierfish (Myripristis vittata) and the luxuriant walls of an undersea grotto offer a perfect composition for a scuba-diving photographer.

B - The alcyonarians some of the most spectacular features of the reef: they create veritable underwater gardens, distinguished by the most spectacular array of colors.

C

C - An enormous array of sea fans (Gorgonia ventalina) extends out from the coral wall, reaching into the ocean water for a distance of over two meters (six feet). At the tip of its branches, a number of feather stars are delicately perched.

D

F

D - *Two grey reef sharks* (Carcharhinus amblyrhynchos) *patrol the reef in search of prey.*

E - *The yellowmask angelfish* (Pomacanthus xanthometopon) *lives alone or in pairs, and it feeds chiefly on sponges.*

F, G - *Bluestriped snappers* (Lutjanus kasmira) *with their distinctive yellow coloring and four light-blue stripes, tend to swim along the reef walls in an incessant search for food.*

E

G

H - *Huge schools of bannerfish* (Heniochus diphreutes) *are one of the most distinctive features of dives on Banana Reef; especially on the northernmost edge of the reef, it is possible to encounter groups made up of over five hundred individuals.*

H

OKOBE THILA - BARRACUDA GIRI

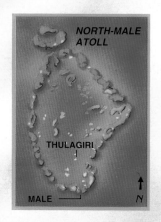

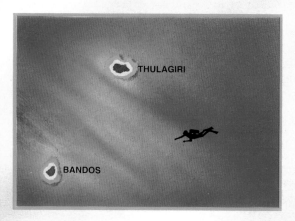

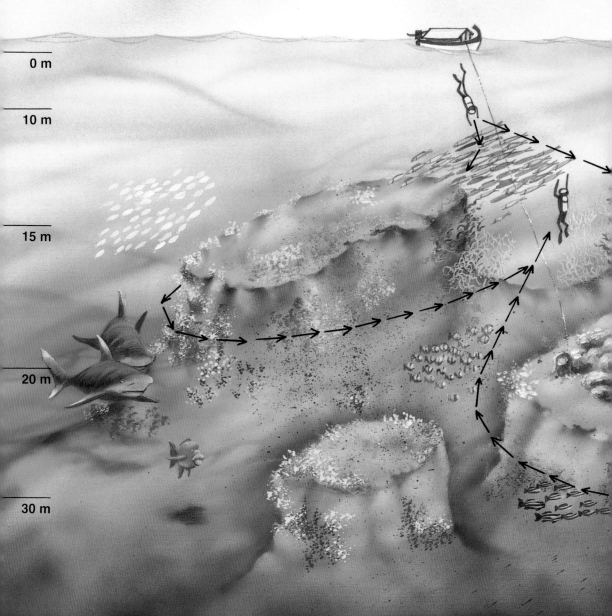

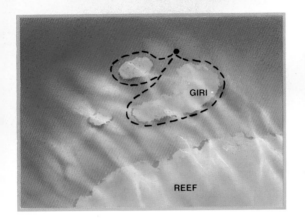

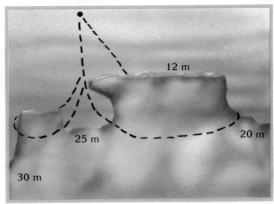

GIRI

REEF

12 m

25 m

30 m

20 m

LOCATION

Barracuda Giri lies in the North-Male Atoll, north-northeast of Bandos and south-southeast of Thulagiri. Both of the *thilas* overlook a reef, and are respectively twelve and fourteen meters (thirty-nine and forty-six feet) deep. The eastern side drops straight down to a depth of thirty meters (a hundred feet), while in all the other directions the seabed runs away at depths ranging from twenty meters (sixty-five feet) to twenty-five meters (just over eighty feet). The reef proper lies just a hundred meters (three hundred thirty feet) further west. The largest of the *thilas* is about eighty meters (262 feet) in length, while the smallest measures about forty meters (131 feet).

When currents are weak, it is possible to swim entirely around both of the *thilas*.

The canyon separating the *thilas* plunges to depths of about twenty-five meters (just over eighty feet) and is about thirty meters (a hundred feet) in width.

A - The batfish (Platax teira) is quite common throughout the archipelago of the Maldives.

B - A number of large specimens of the Oriental grunt (Plectorhynchus orientalis) accompany a scuba diver underwater.

C - Elegant formations of alcyonarians adorn the reef walls; around them turns the incessant whirl of reef life.

D - A splendid carangid, the giant trevally (Caranx ignobilis), plies the waters off Barracuda Giri, glittering with silvery reflections.

E

DIVES

The activity during a dive is concentrated in this spot. Boats usually moor at a permanent mooring hook. Since, in this manner, the responsibility of returning to the boat belongs to the scuba divers, it will be necessary to make a dive against the current; the current reaches its greatest force in the canyon. In the presence of favorable currents, Barracuda Giri boasts some truly spectacular dives; given the conditions, however, only advanced divers should venture on this dive.

E - This startling picture, taken against the light, allows the reader to form an idea of the remarkable size of this gorgonian.

LIFE FORMS

Given the high level of exposure of this site, those who dive here encounter a remarkable abundance of fish. For some years now, in fact, a school of large batfish *(Platax teira)* have lived here, and they are generally encountered near the northern tip of the *thilas*.

There are also large schools of blackspotted sweetlips *(Plectorhynchus picus)* beneath the various projections, and in the waters on the deepest side, barracuda *(Sphyraena sp.)* and other pelagic fish cruise back and forth. Often, whitetip reef sharks *(Carcharhinus albimarginatus)* are sighted. A number of large morays live on the southern side, while on the reef top scorpion fish *(Pterois sp.)* swim to and fro. The canyon is decorated with gorgonians and soft coral, and on the south side grow black coral. Of course, the sociable and cheery humphead wrasse *(Cheilinus undulatus)* can be found here.

SAFETY

As always when the boat is moored, the dive should begin and end on the mooring line. The planning should be such that one first dives against the current and then, toward the end of the dive, when the preassure in the tank is low and energy flags, one returns to the boat with the current in greater safety.

RESPECT FOR THE ENVIRONMENT

Okobe Thila is conveniently and centrally located; for many years, it has been explored by setting out from bases in the southernmost area of the North-Male Atoll. The damage caused in the early years, when scuba divers were not as environmentally aware as they are now, still exists. Contact with the coral must absolutely be avoided, especially in the area where the boat moors below jutting rocks and near narrows. When one swims against the current in the canyon and one is forced to grip onto the coral, try to do so upon dead blocks of coral.

F

PHOTOGRAPHY

In this site, the photographer is presented with many different compositions, ranging from the panoramic shot with a model posing, all the way to macro photographs. Suggested compositions: batfish and sweetlips, with which one also eventually has to deal, if taken against the blue background of the water, make for excellent photographs. Suggested focal lengths: 20- to 15-millimeter.

F - With their slender and aerodynamic shapes, the barracudas (Sphyraena sp.) are undaunted by even the most powerful currents.

G - The emperor angelfish (Pomacanthus imperator) displays one of the most spectacular colorings of the undersea world, its oval body alternating numerous dark-blue and bright-yellow stripes.

H - This picture once again shows us the wealth of underwater life of the seabeds of the Maldives: alcyonarians and sea lilies together form a delicate natural composition.

G

H

NASSIMO-THILA - BLUE SHADOW

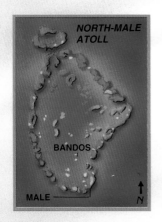

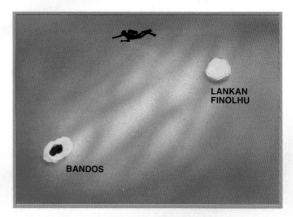

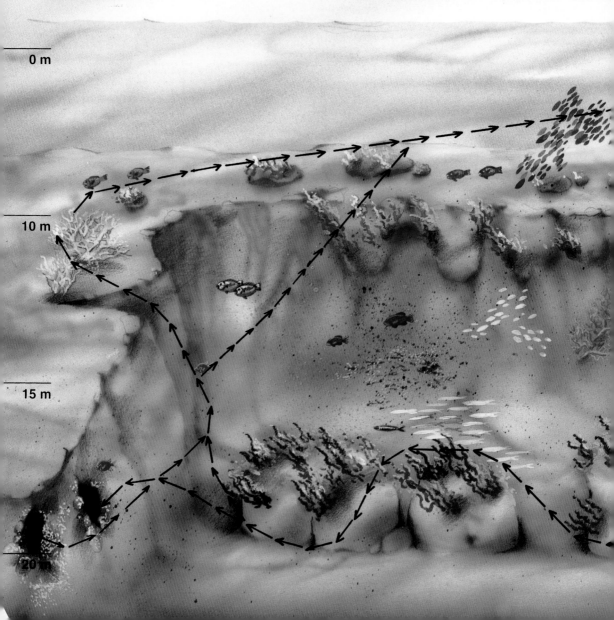

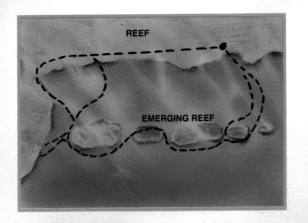

REEF

EMERGING REEF

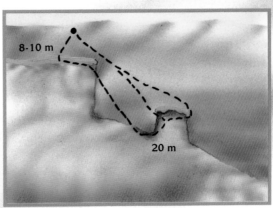

8-10 m

20 m

LOCATION

Blue Shadow is on the east side of the North Male Atoll, inside the barrier reef. Nearby islands are Bandos to the southwest and Lankanfinolhu, directly to the east. The *thila*, which rise to about nine meters (thirty feet) beneath the surface, is many hundreds of meters (many hundreds of yards) in diameter. The site of the dive is on the eastern side of the *thila*.
On the edges of the reef, the seabed plunges down to a depth of about twenty meters (sixty-five feet). From here, enormous blocks of coral rise to almost ten meters (thirty-three feet) beneath the surface. The seascape is

already quite fantastic in and of itself, but the undergrowth of soft corals and the amazing abundance of fish make this place one of the most handsome in the North-Male Atoll.

DIVES

At Blue Shadow one can moor the boat at any of a number of coral blocks. As has been pointed out in the general description of the place, the currents are normally quite strong, especially on the top of the reef. Anyone who dives here should therefore take shelter in the inlets and in the lee of coral formations. Nevertheless, if one knows the place quite well and calculates the currents carefully, one can make a drift dive as well. After the dive, one can surface,

still floating with the current, along the reef or else out to the open water.

LIFE FORMS

The top of the reef is spangled with numerous large blocks of coral, entirely covered with multicolored soft corals, and amidst which swim schools of bluestriped snappers *(Lutjanus kasmira)* and blackspotted sweetlips *(Plectorhynchus picus)*. Here, however, one can see vast quantities of nearly all the species of reef fish present in the Maldives. Moreover, on the rocks jutting from the edges of the reef, grow the extremely rare soft blue corals, in the midst of which a few giant humphead wrasses lurk *(Chelinus undulatus)*, waiting for a chance to accompany a scuba diver on his or her excursions. A common sight amongst the coral blocks is a large barracuda *(Sphyraena sp.)* about 120 centimeters (about four feet) in length, while near the side facing outward, the waters are plied by tuna fish *(Thunnus sp.)* and jacks *(Caranx sp.)*.

SAFETY

This site may be swept by powerful currents. While planning the dive, one should keep in mind that, when one reaches the end of the dive, it will be necessary to return to the point of departure, where the boat is moored above the edge of the reef, which is where the currents are strongest. Therefore, one must make certain that enough air is left in the tanks. It would in any case be best to swim as much as possible in the shelter of the edge of the reef, so as to be able to return to the boat by simply drifting along in the current. If, on the other hand, as we mentioned above, one chooses to do a drift dive, one should bring a parachute, because the three minute safety stop at a depth of five meters (sixteen feet) must be made in the open waters. As for any other drift dive, the crew of the boat should have exact instructions so that they can keep an eye on the drifting buoys.

RESPECT FOR THE ENVIRONMENT

This site is frequented by a great number of scuba divers.
All those who wish to fall under the spell of Blue Shadow must heed the appeal to help, through behavior that shows great respect for the environment, to keep this natural wonder intact; one should not touch or pet any fish, not even the humphead wrasse *(Cheilinus undulatus)* which may at times even seem intrusive.

PHOTOGRAPHY

Because of the abundant soft corals, this place seems designed specifically as a background for seascape photography.
If one wishes to include a scuba diver in one's shot, then one should make use of a super-wide-angle lens. For the photography of schools of fish atop the reef, as well, shorter focal lengths, such as a 20-millimeter lens, can be useful. And if one plans to take photographs of individual fish or soft corals, then Blue Shadow is truly a photographer's paradise.
Suggested composition: Jutting coral masses with multicolored soft corals and a scuba diver hovering in the watery blue background.

A - A scuba diver, pulled by a scooter, loops around a dense school of bluestripe snappers (Lutjanus kasmira).

B - A humphead wrasse (Cheilinus undulatus) curves tightly near the reef, on the walls of which grow the very rare blue coral.

C - The beauty of the corals is equalled only by their fragility, and so scuba divers should be particularly careful to refrain from touching them: it takes only the slightest impact for the work that millions of animals have carried out over the centuries and millennia to be completely and irrevocably eliminated.

D - A small compact school of onespot snappers (Lutjanus monostigma) patrols the reef, in search of their customary prey.

E - The presence of this green alcyonarian constitute a remarkable feature of diving at Nassimo Thila, which, because of the wealth of animal life and the remarkable flora, is certainly one of the most interesting and spectacular sites in the archipelago of the Maldives.

F - A bluefin trevally (Caranx melampygus) darts quickly away from the photographer's lens.

G - The rays of the sun glitter off the back of a large barracuda (Sphyraena sp.), just over a meter in length. The larger specimens rarely live in a group, and prefer to do their hunting on their own.

37

TAMBURUDU - H.P. REEF

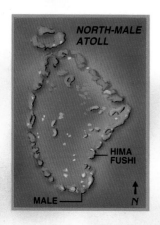

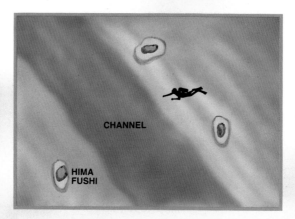

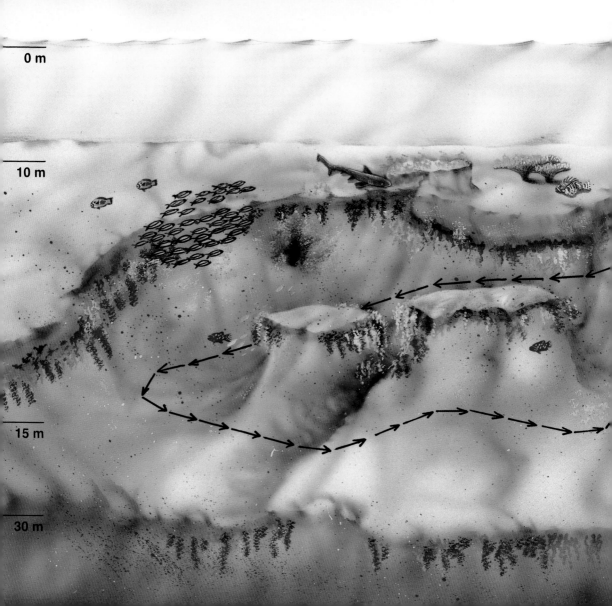

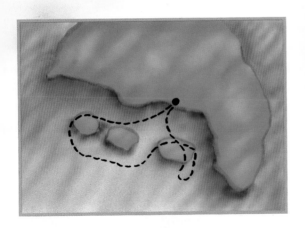

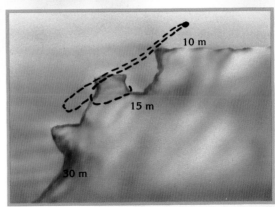

10 m

15 m

30 m

A - With their unmistakable silohuettes, a great many spotted eagle rays (Aetobatus narinari) *swim majestically through the open ocean.*

B - *The unfailing presence of powerful currents along the reefs of Tamburudu has encouraged the proliferation of manicolored alcyonarian.*

C - *A tawny nurse shark (Nebrius ferrugineus) sleeps on the seabed, its snout hidden in the rocks, waiting for the night and the nocturnal hunt.*

B

C

LOCATION

Tamburudu lies on the east side of the North-Male Atoll.
The site of the dive is located in the channel that separates the nearby islands of Himafushi and Girifushi from that of Tamburudu. These are three enormous coral formations, which loom up near the walls of the channel, and upon which grow extremely luxuriant soft corals of every color, chiefly because of the virtually incessant main currents.
Nonetheless, at least when the movement of the water is not excessively disturbed, this is an excellent site for diving, both because of the inlets in the reef wall and because of the presence of coral formations.
The peak of the reef lies at a

D

good ten meters (thirty-three feet) of depth, and from here the seabed drops nearly vertically. After a sort of saddle at a depth of about fifteen meters (about fifty feet), the three coral blocks split up over a length of about one hundred fifty meters (about five hundred feet), also at a depth ranging from thirteen to fifteen meters (forty to fifty feet).
The northernmost of the three is halted by a large fissure, called the "Chimney," where soft corals seen against the light offer an excellent subject for photographers.
Facing the channel, the seabed drops directly to depths of thirty meters (fifty feet) and more.

D - *This panoramic photograph shows us the crest of the reef, which lies about ten meters (thirty-three feet) under the surface.*

DIVES

In the presence of powerful currents, the simplest way of exploring H.P. Reef is on a drift dive: one simply lets oneself be carried in by the current, and then one can tour freely in the shelter of the coral blocks. With average or weak currents, the boat can be moored on the spot with a line, and then one must plan carefully so that the dive ends in the same place from which one set out. As mentioned previously, the top of the reef is ten meters (thirty-three feet) beneath the surface, and therefore it is necessary to do the three minutes of safety-stop at a depth of five meters (about sixteen feet) by holding onto the mooring line.

LIFE FORMS

As mentioned above, the enormous explosion of multicolored soft coral is particularly decorative here, but at the edge of the reef one can also see schools of bluestriped snappers *(Lutjanus kasmira)*, while amongst the table corals it is possible to find the entire range of marine life, such as crocodile fish *(Cociella crocodilus)* and scorpion fish *(Pterois sp.)*. It is also fairly common to see nurse sharks *(Nebrius ferrugineus)* lurking amidst the coral blocks at the reef top. In the open ocean, behind or in front of the coral blocks, eagle rays *(Aetobatus narinari)* and large tuna fish *(Thunnus sp.)* come and go. Sea turtles *(Eretmochelys imbricata)* can also often be seen.

SAFETY

For the safety-stop in the open water, quite necessary during drift dives, but also in order to allow the teams that have moved along the channel or on top of the reef can be spotted by the boat, the parachute is absolutely necessary.

RESPECT FOR THE ENVIRONMENT

One must be especially careful at the reef top, upon which large coral tables are found. As on any other place, divers should keep an appropriate distance so as not to damage the coral. While swimming near jutting rocks and caves, one should be particularly careful with one's flippers, to prevent any contact with soft corals.

PHOTOGRAPHY

For taking seascape photographs with a full-format fisheye lenses or with super-wide-angle lenses, this place is unbeatable. Soft corals absorb much more light than hard corals, and so a great deal of light is needed.

E - Nature generates veritable artistic masterpieces in the life forms of the sea bottom.

F - A coral grouper (Cephalopholis miniata) signals with the position of its gills its willingness to entrust itself to the care of the busy cleaner wrasse.

G, H - Sponges, corals, sea anemones, starfish, and multicolored fish all join together to form an incredible array of hues, that no painted could dream of reproducing.

RASFAREE KANDU - RASFAREE CORNER

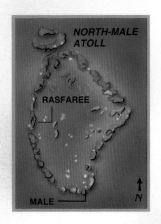

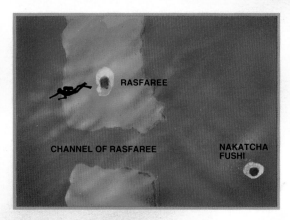

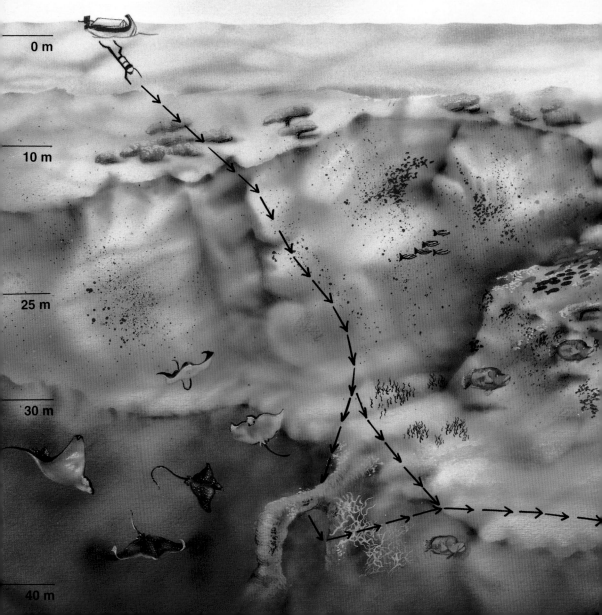

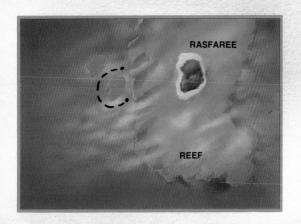

RASFAREE

REEF

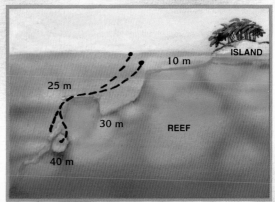

10 m

25 m

30 m

40 m

ISLAND

REEF

A

B

C

D

E

LOCATION

Rasfaree Corner is on North-Male Atoll, outside of the barrier reef, near the northern edge of the channel of Rasfaree. Nearby islands are Rasfaree to the north and Nakatchafushi to the southwest. The place described here is not directly on the reef itself, but is rather a colossal coral foundation standing before the reef, which barely rises to a depth of twenty-two meters (seventy feet) beneath the surface. On the eastern side, this foundation drops sheer away to depths of thirty meters (one hundred feet) and more.

DIVES

This site can be reached on a drift dive. The currents must be tracked with care in order to reach the best location. It is therefore necessary to plan one's dive so as to begin by exploring the deeper section of the place. There should be enough air left at this point to explore the interesting reef-top.

LIFE FORMS

Rasfaree owes its renown chiefly to its sharks. Depending on how the currents are running, one can encounter entire schools of fairly large grey reef sharks (Carcharhinus amblyrhynchos), and often very large oceanic whitetip sharks (Carcharhinus longimanus) are spotted as well. Above the reef, on the other hand, are the whitetip (Carcharhinus albimarginatus) and blackfin sharks (Carcharhinus melanopterus),

A typical inhabitant of the tropical sea, the coral grouper (Cephalopholis miniata) is characterized by a garish orange-red coloring, with numerous tiny ocellated blue splotches.

B - Redmouth groupers (Aethaloperca rogaa), too, make use of cleaner fish to rid themselves of parasites.

C, D - In the waters off Rasfaree Kandu it is fairly common to encounter grey reef sharks (Carcharhinus amblyrhynchos, which sometimes gather in fairly sizable groups.

E - Coral colonies are the foundation of life on the reef, inasmuch as they provide nutrition and protection to the smaller fish that find an ideal habitat on the coral reef.

F - For more than two hundred million years, sea turtle have been tirelessly plying the routes of the ocean; from the time of the dinosaurs, their structure has changed only to a tiny degree. The loveliest turtle of them all is without a doubt the hawksbill turtle (Eretmochelys imbricata), which glides through the underwater depths with elegant swipes of its flippers.

as well as the occasional sea turtle *(Eretmochelys imbricata)*. In deeper waters, i.e., near the sheer drop of the wall, a group of large eagle rays *(Aetobatus narinari)* often swims by, while those who look toward the open ocean from here can also see a number of other large pelagic fish. Lastly, in the presence of powerful currents, this place becomes a necessary point of passage for very large fish.

SAFETY

In the presence of weak currents, even the least experienced of scuba divers can dive at Rasfaree, as long as they are accompanied by a guide. Those who wish to

G - Just beyond the coral reef, where the reef wall drops away into the deep blue waters, it is not rare to see a large group of spotted eagle rays (Aetobatus narinari) swim by in procession.

H - Where the current is particularly powerful, it is possible to encounter pelagic fish of considerable size. In this picture, a dense school of bigeye trevallies (Caranx sexfasciatus) flees as the scuba divers approach.

to find the dive team and to pick them up.

RESPECT FOR THE ENVIRONMENT

As in all sites where one dives in the presence of powerful currents, it is best to keep an adequate distance from the reef. One should be particularly careful when surfacing near projections, lest one damage gorgonians and alcyonarians with one's fins.

PHOTOGRAPHY

In this spot, fish of considerable size present themselves to the waiting photographer. The ideal lenses for taking pictures of entire sharks — which can be as long as two meters, or six-and-a-half feet — at a distance of two or three meters, or six-and-a-half feet to ten feet, are 24- or 28-millimeter lenses.
One should avoid using flashes in "TTL modus" or "full".
Since sharks should be shot with the open ocean as a background, one should use a strobe on half, or even a quarter of full power.
If in fact the flash were to prove to be too powerful, the body of the shark would be overexposed and the particles in suspension in the water would appear in the photograph as white dots, the so-called "back scatters".

dive alone should be advanced divers. Since it is necessary to move long distances at depths ranging from twenty to twenty-five meters (sixty-five to eighty feet), one must learn to manage one's air consumption on the way so as to have enough left to finish the dive by exploring the reef-top. The eastern side drops straight away to truly considerable depths, a proper buoyancy control is important and one should respect the limits of depth. When there are stronger currents, one could be swept for considerable distances over the top or along the sides of the reef, and so it will be necessary to bring a parachute, in order to make it easier for the boat

KUDA FARU - SADDLE

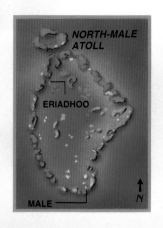

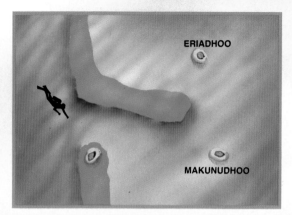

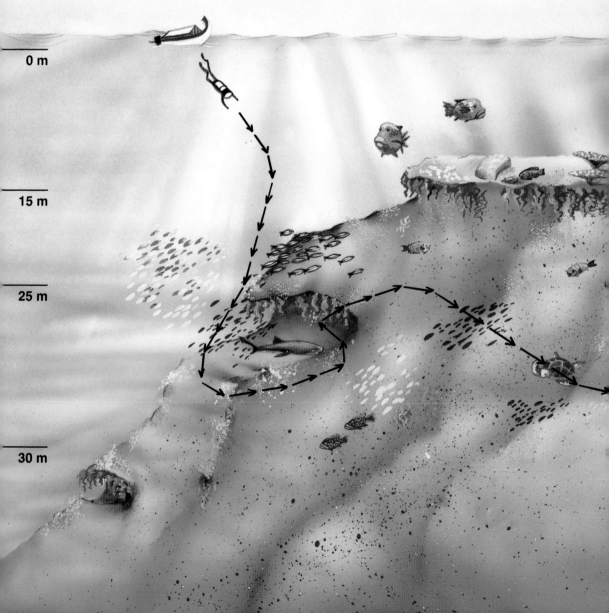

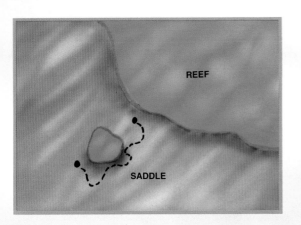

REEF

SADDLE

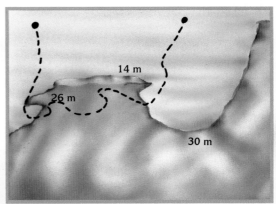

14 m

26 m

30 m

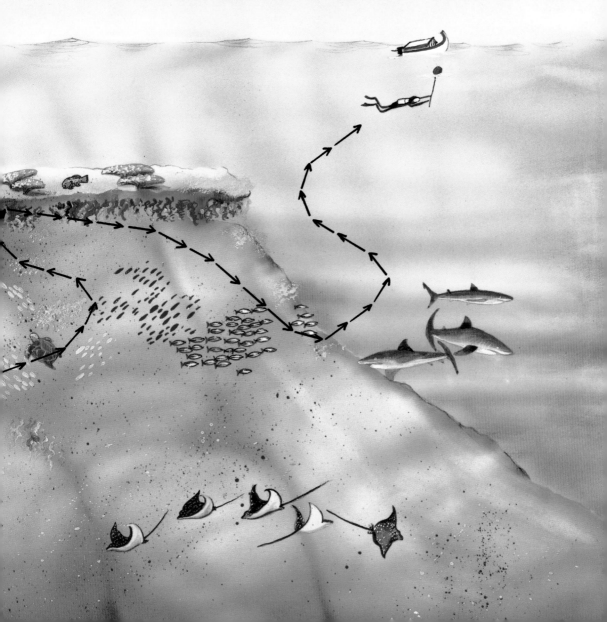

LOCATION

Saddle lies on the western side of the North-Male Atoll. The closest islands are Eriadhoo to the north and Makunudhoo to the south-southeast. The term saddle describes this reef very well; unlike the classic *thila*, it does not drop away into the deep, but rather it slopes gently down in an almost symmetrical manner. The upper section of the saddle is relatively flat and rises to a depth of just thirteen meters (about forty-three feet) beneath the surface. To the southwest, south, and southeast, the slopes drop away to considerable depths. Particularly noteworthy is the large cavern that lies at a depth of twenty-six meters (eighty-five feet). The saddle is a large coral block that extends for over one thousand meters (thirty-three hundred feet) in the channel of Makunudhoo.

DIVES

Kuda Faru is a site suitable for scuba divers with average to high degrees of experience. On the saddle there is always current of some sort, and at certain points that current can become very powerful. Depending on whether one dives with incoming or outgoing current, visibility can also vary considerably.
As in all channels, the best conditions are found with inflowing current. This site is only appropriate for drift dives.

LIFE FORMS

The location of the saddle on the interior of a current-rich channel is the reason why this place can boast a population of soft corals that is far above the average. On the upper part of this reef, enormous table corals grow. Of course, there had to be sharks, and they can be encountered regularly at the corners most heavily pounded by the currents. Here there are grey reef sharks *(Carcharhinus amblyrhynchos)*, while on the plateau near the cavern, one can often find nurse sharks *(Nebrius ferrugineus)*. When diving on Saddle, it is a good idea to keep a very alert eye

toward the open waters. There is a very good possibility of spotting a group of eagle rays *(Aetobatus narinari)*.Here, large schools of red soldierfish *(Myripristis murdjan)* and sweetlips *(Plectorhynchus sp.)*, while sea turtles *(Eretmochelys imbricata)* are not uncommon. Large humphead wrasses *(Cheilinus undulatus)* also regularly accompany the scuba divers.

SAFETY

As we have already pointed out, in some places the saddle drops down to a considerable depth. Despite any enthusiasm that might sweep one away, one

should not dive past the depth limits. The great size of the reef means that some dives must be conditioned by the ease with which one can orient oneself there underwater. It is therefore important to discuss the plan of the dive thoroughly, so that one is completely able to find the details of the site, such as the cavern or the corners occupied by the sharks.
The upper section of the reef lies thirteen meters (about forty-three feet) beneath the surface, and therefore the safety stop of three minutes at a depth of five meters (sixteen feet) should be made in the open water.
It is helpful to use the parachute so that the boat's crew is easily able to track the movements of the scuba divers when they are inside the channel.

A - A dead branch of black coral has been entirely covered with sea anemones, sponges, and mollusks.

B - The oriental grunt (Plectorhynchus orientalis), *which is particularly common throughout the archipelago, live in small groups in the area around the reef or near large coral formations.*

C - This macrophotography reveals the delicate perfection of a branch of alcyonarian.

D - As one can easily gather from its large eyes, the soldierfish (Myripristis vittata) is prevalently nocturnal.

E - A tawny nurse shark (Nebrius ferrugineus) rests in a grotto, in the company of a small sharksucker (Echeneis naucrates), fastened to its head.

F - A number of feather stars (Oligometra serripinna), perched on the branches of a gorgonia, filter the plankton that is swept in by the currents.

G - A blackspotted stingray (Taeniura melanospilos) swims with elegant strokes along the sandy seabed.

H - Just a few yards beneath the surface, an alcyonarian (Sarcophyton sp.), its polyps expanded, filter-feeds on microorganisms carried by the current.

RESPECT FOR THE ENVIRONMENT

Special attention should be paid whenever one is moving along the slopes of the reef in the presence of strong currents. In such conditions, to avoid damaging corals, it would be wise to keep a sufficient distance from the reef.
Even with strong currents, one can hover in place, if one takes shelter behind some large coral block.

PHOTOGRAPHY

For an environmental photographer, the saddle offers ideas for any focal length.
The wide-angle lens is always useful. For shots of individual fish, and for macro shots, however, it is important that the current not be too strong.
The luxuriant growth of soft corals on the coral blocks makes for certain photographs with remarkable colors. For shots of this sort, however, one need not rely solely on the wide-angle lens. It is a good idea to take some detailed photographs, or even some macro shots of these structures.
Suggested compositions:
The school of red soldierfish *(Myripristis sp.)*, photographed against the deep blue of the water, will produce a very high contrast photograph.
In order to obtain a correct reproduction of the red of the fish, however, one should get as close as possible, and in any case to less than a meter-and-a-half (five feet).

E

F

G

D

H
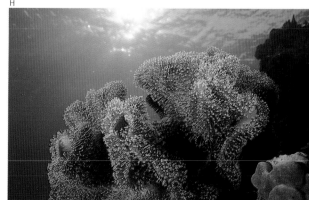

MEERUFENFUSHI - STAIRS

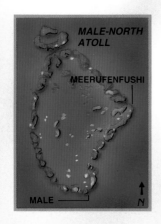

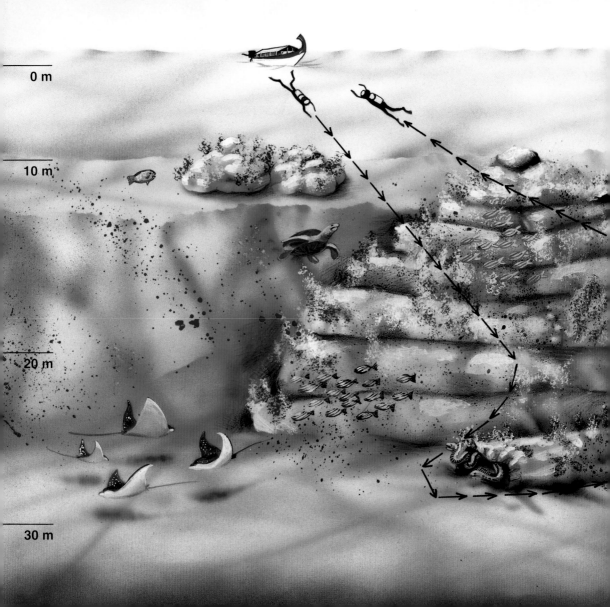

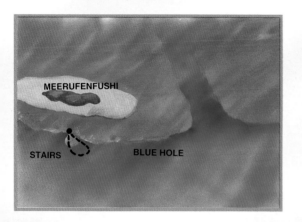

MEERUFENFUSHI

STAIRS   BLUE HOLE

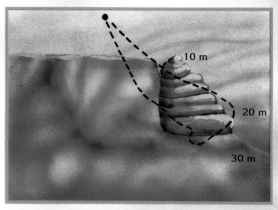

10 m

20 m

30 m

LOCATION

The site of the dive is on the east side of the North-Male Atoll, outside of the barrier reef. Nearby islands are Dhiffushi and Meerufenfushi. The Stairs is a giant mushroom coral the shape of which is reminiscent of a flight of stairs that descends from a depth of ten meters (thirty-three feet) to a depth of twenty-five meters (eighty-two feet). At the edge of this same reef, rise a number of mushroom corals similar to "The Stairs," although they are smaller in size.

DIVES

"The Stairs" is a place ideally suited for any and all levels of experience and skill because, lying as it does at a considerable distance from the channel of Dhiffushi, it is absolutely free from powerful currents.
Scuba divers can enter the water from their boats, explore the site, and then end their dive along the edges of the reef.

LIFE FORMS

This site is characterized by an enormous abundance of fish. Along the steps gather in good order a great many oriental sweetlips *(Plectorhynchus orientalis)* and snappers *(Lutjanus kasmira)*.
At the edges of the reef, at the base of the so-called stairs, one finds mainly whitetip reef sharks *(Carcharhinus albimarginatus)*, although it is common to see sea turtles *(Eretmochelys imbricata)* as well. Also at the base of "The Stairs" it is worth one's while to look beyond the sandy seabed that slopes slightly towards the depths of the clear blue open ocean: rocked by the slight current, there are a number of eagle rays *(Aetobatus narinari)* that gather here. Also at the edges of the reef, inside and beneath the mushroom corals, live a number of large morays *(Gymnothorax javanicus)*, which at times peer out of their dens, in some cases in pairs.
And the steps are also decorated by marvelous soft corals.

SAFETY

To judge from currents and depths, the level of skill required for this dive is elementary. However, since the top of the reef lies at some ten meters (or about thirty-three feet) beneath the surface of the water, it is necessary to do three minutes of safety stop at a depth of five meters (about sixteen feet) drifting in the open water with a parachute.

RESPECT FOR THE ENVIRONMENT

Mushroom corals are not endowed with the well defined structures found in other species; rather they have flat, rock-like surfaces.
Divers must nonetheless keep in mind that these house the coral polyps; therefore, even if bumping against or grazing these corals does not produce immediately visibile damage, the meautuses in which the polyps live may be harmed.

PHOTOGRAPHY

During the course of this dive, one can make use of any focal length: from super-wide-angle lenses in order to take panoramic shots of scuba divers to the wide-angle 20-millimeter lens to capture a fellow diver half-hidden by a school of fish, all the way to focal lengths of 50- or 35-millimeters, for photographs of individual fish and for portraits. Suggested shots: A school of blackspotted sweetlips *(Plectorhynchus picus)* head on, with a scuba diver in the background.

A - Around the island of Meerufenfushi, the various depths of the seabed create enchanting contrasts and harmonious nuances of color.

B - A scuba diver swims in the midst of a silvery cloud of slender sweepers (Parapriacanthus guentheri).

C - This school of oriental grunts (Plectorhynchus orientalis) hovers at the base of a giant coral mushroom, commonly referred to as "Stairs".

D - At the end of the dive, it is a good idea to allow oneself to be carried by the current along the length of the wall of the reef.

E - Two small Clark's anemonefish (Amphiprion clarkii) peep out from amidst the tentacles of the host sea anemone.

F - The coloring of the yellowhead butterflyfish (Chaetodon xanthocephalus) is distinguished by delicate shades of color, far different from the garish hues of the fish that belong to its species.

HELENGELI THILA

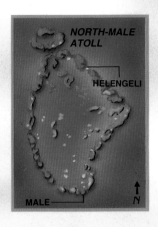

NORTH-MALE
ATOLL

HELENGELI

MALE

N

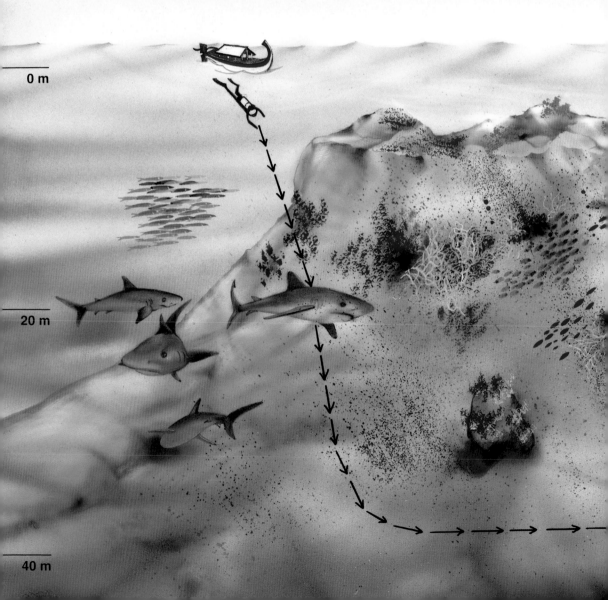

0 m

20 m

40 m

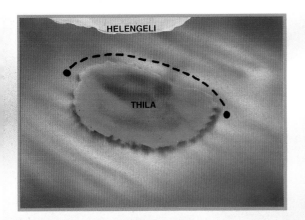

HELENGELI

THILA

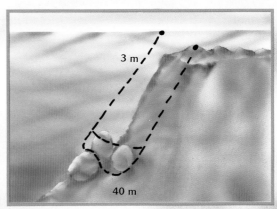

3 m

40 m

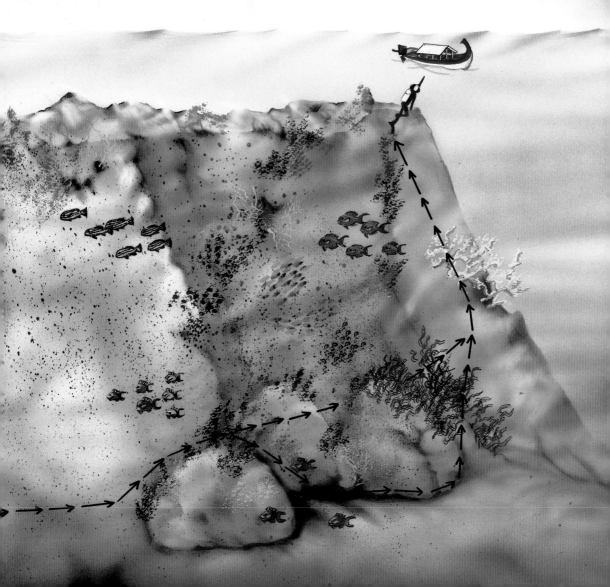

LOCATION

Helengeli lies on the northeast side of the North-Male Atoll. The diving site consists of a shallows that is located in the channel between the islands of Helengeli and the reef of Maifhalhu. The *thila* extends for a distance of one hundred fifty meters (about five hundred feet) from east to west and, rising from a seabed forty meters (one hundred thirty feet) deep, towers to within eight or ten meters (twenty-six to thirty-three feet) beneath the surface. The reef walls

A, B, C, D - In the western section of the thila, *along the reef walls, a great many grottoes open up, completely covered by vividly colored soft corals, and by huge sea fans.*

drop away sheer to the sandy bottom of the channel. The most interesting part is the one facing north, because it is riddled with large fissures teeming with alcyonarians of all colors; near the shallows, there are mushroom corals standing six to seven meters (twenty to twenty-three feet) tall; around these there is such a teeming profusion of life that it is difficult to think of anything comparable.

DIVES

In order to enjoy the best conditions of visibility it is best to make one's drift dive with the incoming current, taking care to ensure that the current is not too powerful, otherwise because the shallows are not at all long, the dive will only last for a few minutes.
The dhoni will convey the divers to a distance of thirty meters (a hundred feet) to the east of the shallows, so that there is plenty of time, even for the least accomplished of the divers, to go as deep as they like at the beginning of the *thila*.
The safety stop should be made at five meters, or eight feet, in open waters.

LIFE FORMS

This point is also called "Barracuda Pass", because it is common to encounter a school of barracuda *(Sphyraena sp.)* of considerable size at the summit of the shallows. Given the nature of the fish, it is also possible to spot tuna *(Thunnus sp.)*, grey reef sharks *(Carcharhinus amblyrhynchos)*, and eagle rays *(Aetobatus narinari)*, and on the bottom blackspotted rays *(Taeniura melanospilos)*.
Around the isolated mushrooms, there are schools of surgeonfish *(Acanthurus sp.)* and sweetlips *(Plectorhynchus sp.)*.
The western part, where the first dive ends, at a depth of between twenty and thirty meters (sixty-five and a hundred feet), opens out into splendid grottoes full of great gorgonian fans *(Gorgonia ventalina)*.

E

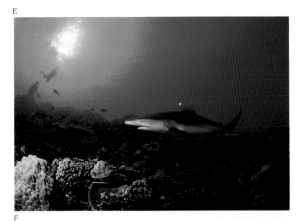

E - A grey reef shark (Carcharhinus amblyrhynchos) patrols the reef in a menacing manner.

F - Adult specimens of the great barracuda (Sphyraena barracuda) grow to a considerable size, with lengths of up to two meters (six-and-a-half feet).

F

G

H

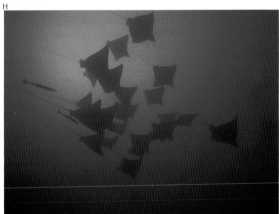

SAFETY AND RESPECT FOR THE ENVIRONMENT

Inasmuch as safety is concerned, one should follow the cautionary rules that apply to every dive, and be sure to follow the guidelines of ecological awareness that should be followed in any dealings with nature.

PHOTOGRAPHY

Using wide-angle lenses will offer an opportunity to shoot in mixed light with the fans of gorgonians in the foreground and a scuba diver in the distance. Another subject would be the schools of fish, which should be shot with 20- and 28-mm lenses.

I

G - The yellow boxfish (Ostracion cubicus) lives chiefly in the area around the reef. Common in the Indian Ocean and the Pacific Indian, when it feels threatened it produces a toxic substance.

H - Spotted eagle rays (Aetobatus narinari) are certainly some of the most alluring creatures of the

underwater world; they can grow to be more than two meters (six-and-a-half feet) wide and two-and-a-half meters (eight feet) in overall length.

I - Blackspotted stingrays (Taeniura melanospilos) are exceedingly sociable animals. They are not aggressive, and they use the venomous spines at the base of their tail strictly for self-defense.

GAAFARU - *SEAGULL WRECK*

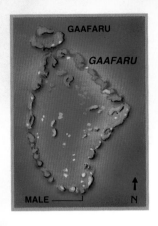

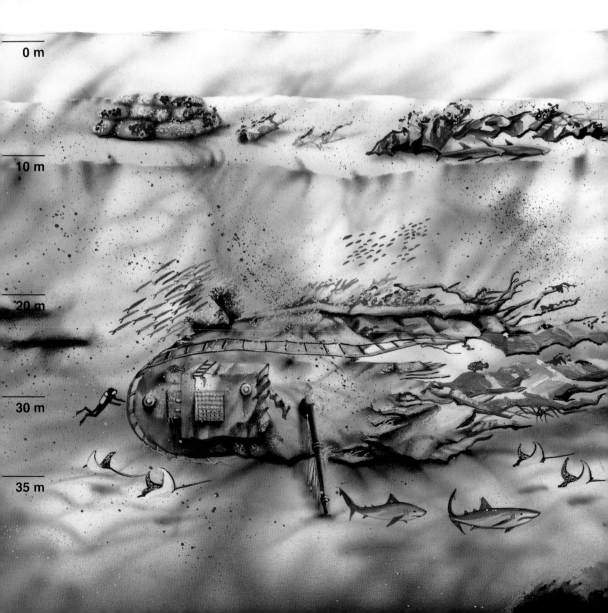

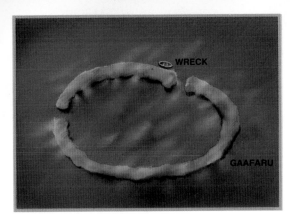

WRECK

GAAFARU

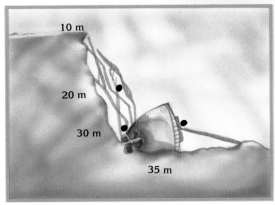

10 m

20 m

30 m

35 m

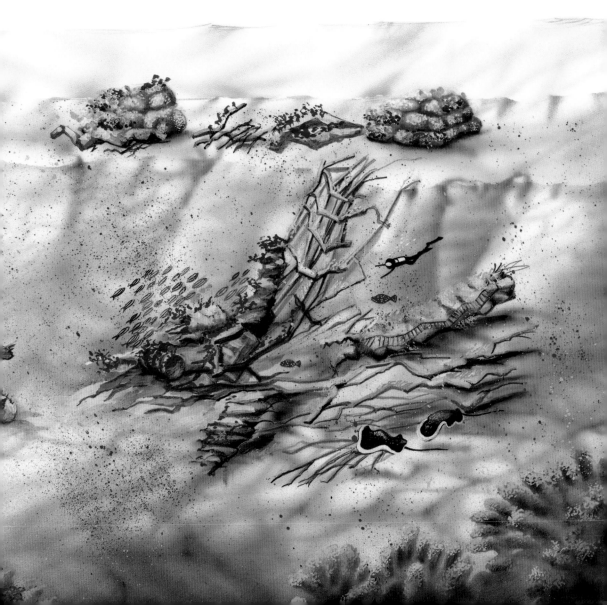

A

LOCATION

The wreck lies near the outer wall of the reef to the north of the atoll of Gaafaru, half a mile to the west of the Invai Kandu, the northern entrance to the atoll of Gaafaru. Even on the top of the reef, which ranges in depth from six to ten meters (from twenty to about thirty-three feet), it is possible to see scattered fragments of the wreck.

The true main body of the wreck is completely split into two parts. The bowsprit, of which only the ribbing survives, lies at a right angle near the scarp of the reef. The rear section of the wreck, on the other hand, lies parallel to the reef with its keel pointing south, at a depth of thirty meters (one hundred feet).

A - All that remains of the Seagull's *bow is a skeletal structure, resting on the reef. This metal ribbing provides an excellent backdrop for photographs taken against the light.*

B

B, C - Many fish have taken the shipwreck as their home; among them are pesci pipistrello (Platax teira) and coral groupers (Cephalopholis miniata).

HISTORY

Little is known with certainty about the *Seagull,* the port from which she hailed, her route, and her loss. In one report, she is described as a sailing ship that made her last voyage in 1879, from London to Calcutta. This wreck, however, was a steamboat. Circumstantial evidence, therefore, contradicts both the origin and the name of the ship; all the same, it is a wonderful wreck to explore.

C

D - Inside the sunken ship, one can still see old bottles of wine and soda water, covered with coral concretions.

E - Practically unrecognizable, and now part of nature, a porthole gapes open in the hull of the Seagull.

F - Among the inhabitants of the sunken ship there is also a splendid emperor angelfish (Pomacanthus imperator).

DIVES

Outside of the reef, precisely on the spot where the ship went down and therefore not far from the broad channel, the currents are almost always very powerful. If the divers will be starting from a safari-boat, then it is necessary to wait for the right moment, because exploring the *Seagull* is enjoyable only when the currents are weak. The simplest way of approaching the place is with a drift dive; it is extremely easy to pick out the spot, even from a distance, with all the wreckage that surrounds it. This sort of dive is at any rate usually reserved only for scuba divers at an advanced level.

D

Usually, during the winter, with the northeastern monsoon, the prevailing current runs from west to east, and so one always begins the dive at no less than a distance of twenty or thirty meters (sixty-six to one hundred feet) from some wreckage that can be glimpsed from the surface, looking toward the reef. In this way, one is tugged along gently toward the part that lies against the scarp, after exploring this, one can dive down toward the ship's stern, which is certainly the most interesting part. Returning to the surface by following a diagonal running along the wall, between depths of twenty-five and fifteen meters (eighty and fifty feet), one can find a number of horizontal crevices in the reef, forming small grottoes where enormous schools of soldierfish *(Myripristis sp.)* take refuge, along with colorful groupers *(Cephalopholis miniata)* and stingrays *(Taeniura melanospilos)* that sleep on the seabed. Near the propeller, between the structures of the ship and the seabed, there is a large den of a blackspotted moray *(Gymnothorax favagineus)* which is curious enough to emerge frequently at the sight of scuba divers.

LIFE FORMS

Even though the most important feature of this dive consists of the excitement of exploring the wreck itself, a certain amount of attention should also be devoted to the life forms to be found on this artificial reef. Among the wreckage that is scattered across the top and the slopes of the reef, a number of nurse sharks *(Nebrius ferrugineus)* can be found, while tens of thousands of *Anthias (Pseudanthias squamipinnis)* crowd the ribbing of what was once the bowsprit. A great many pelagic fish, such as jacks *(Caranx sp.)*, barracudas *(Sphyraena sp.)*, and even eagle rays *(Aetobatus narinari)* and grey reef sharks *(Carcharhinus amblyrhynchos)*, constantly patrol the fragments of the stern that lie at the base of the reef.

SAFETY

The currents, which can be extremely powerful outside of the reef, make it impossible to remain undisturbed in the wreck, and it is therefore absolutely necessary to keep it in mind. Make one's way into the stern of the wreck, at a depth of thirty meters (one hundred feet), one should be quite cautious, inasmuch as a great many passages are narrow and are blocked by metal fragments. It is especially easy to hurt oneself on one of the sharp metal spikes that protrude from the framework of the bowsprit. The normal dive plan, where possible, should include a preliminary exploration of the part of the wreck that lies deepest, and should then rise along the skeletal bowsprit, ending at the top of the reef itself. Because of the danger of cuts on metal spikes, one should wear protective gloves.

RESPECT FOR THE ENVIRONMENT

Ships that have sunk over the course of the years have been transformed into artificial reefs. Therefore the same rules apply that would be observed on a real coral reef.

PHOTOGRAPHY

In order to fit the largest possible portion of the wreck into the photograph, it is necessary to make use — if possible — of a full-format fisheye lens. Super-wide-angle lenses, too, with focal lengths of 14 or 15 millimeters, are also quite useful. Suggested shots: rudder and propeller against the light blue backdrop of the water; the skeleton of the bowsprit with a scuba diver seen against the light.

LHAVIYANI ATOLL - *FELIVARU*

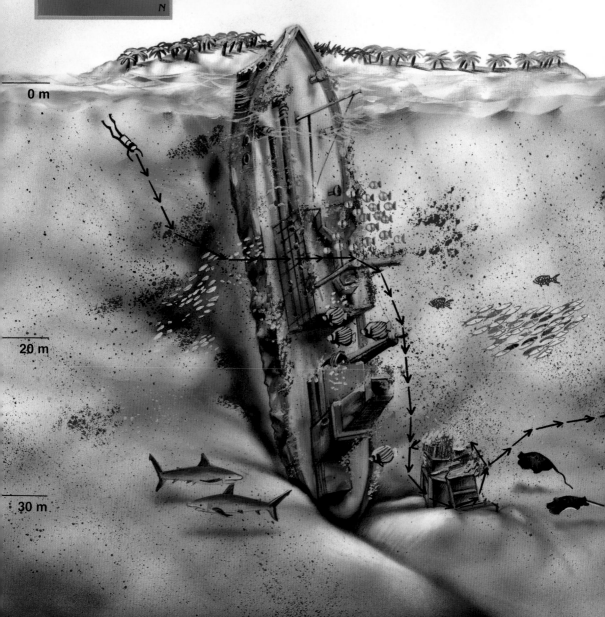

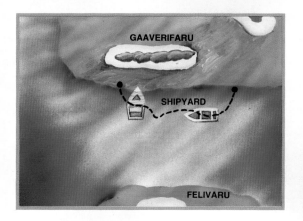

GAAVERIFARU

SHIPYARD

FELIVARU

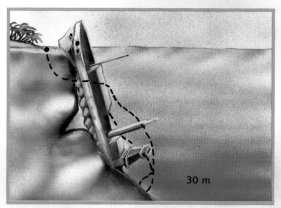

30 m

A

LOCATION

The two wrecks of Felivaru are located in the western section of the atoll of Lhaviyani, inside of the channel that separates the islands of Felivaru and Gaaverifaru. They are easy to find because the bowsprit of one of the wrecks rises five meters (sixteen feet) out of the water. Both lie on a seabed thirty meters (one hundred feet) down: the first (the one that sticks out of the water) of them has its stern on the seabed, and the starboard side leaning against the wall of the pass, while the second one, which had been vertical until the fall of 1992, when a violent storm caused it to settle to the seabed on its port side. The two ships lie about thirty meters (one hundred feet) one from the other.

B

C

D

E

F

A - The entry point can be easily identified by the bow of one of the two wrecks, which sticks some five meters, or sixteen feet, out of the water.

B, C - Both of the wrecks of Felivaru are covered with large alcyonarians that, over time, have transformed the metal structures.

D - An emperor angelfish (Pomacanthus imperator), accompanied by a school of scalefin Anthias (Pseudanthias squamipinnis), swims over the deck of one of the two wrecks, which has since became a spectacular garden of coral.

E - The spectral silhouette of the sunken ship stands out against the dark blue of the ocean waters.

F - A group of batfish (Platax teira) drifts with the current over the main deck.

G - Dense schools of slender sweepers (Parapriacanthus guentheri) swim on the interior of the wreck, scattering silvery reflections.

H - A coral grouper (Cephalopholis miniata), inquisitive about the presence of a photographer, peers from the safe haven of the sunken ship.

I - The garish coloring of the Anthias (Pseudanthias squamipinnis), sponges, and alcyonarians with their lively shapes and hues have reduced the level of tragic drama that inevitably hovers around a wreck.

HISTORY

These two refrigerator ships of Japanese registration were sunk by their owner for no particular reason in 1980 with a full cargo still on board.

DIVES

It is best to dive inward in order to have clearer water. The dhoni will not anchor. The scuba divers enter the water close to the reef, thirty meters (a hundred feet) up-current from the wreck, and they reach the area that is unbuffeted by current as it is in the shelter of the enormous structure of the ship. After exploring the holds and the outside of the first wreck, one drifts with the current to the second wreck and, after thoroughly observing the second one as well, one surfaces moving diagonally along the wall.

LIFE FORMS

This is certainly one of the most colorful and beautiful dives in the Maldives. The wrecks by now are entirely covered with coral and alcyonarians, around which swims every species of tropical reef fish. The coral is intact because on the atoll of Lhaviyani there is only one tourist resort (Kureddu) which offers only one dive a week to the wrecks, with the intention of thus preserving them. The best way to reach the area is on a safari boat. Within the structures of the boats swim millions of glass-fish *(Parapriacanthus guentheri)*, and it is possible to see entire families of emperor angelfish *(Pomacanthus imperator)*. Around the once vertical wreck hovers a school of batfish *(Platax teira)*, and one can get close enough to them to touch them. Inside of the stern hold, which lies on the seabed, one frequently encounters a large nurse shark *(Nebrius ferrugineus)* that sleeps in the shelter of the sheet metal. The distinctive characteristic of the other wreck is that a great many morays *(Gymnothorax sp.)* peep out of the portholes. Since the two wrecks lie in a pass, it is possible to encounter such pelagic fish as tunas *(Thunnus sp.)*, jacks *(Caranx sp.)*, and grey reef sharks *(Carchahinus amblyrhynchos)*.

SAFETY

The location and the depth of the wrecks make this a fairly simple dive, as long as the currents are not too strong. The part of the ship occupied by holds should only be explored by advanced divers, with a great deal of experience, and with a good flashlight. When emerging from the water, it is wise to swim out at least twenty meters (sixty-six feet) from the reef, in order to help the boat to maneuver.

RESPECT FOR THE ENVIRONMENT

Shipwrecks are completely encrusted with life forms, and it is therefore best to refrain from putting one's weight upon them or from touching anything. It is in any case a bad idea to wear protective gloves, and if the checks in advance where he puts his hands, he is certain not to destroy inadvertently a fragile coral formation that has taken years to grow.

PHOTOGRAPHY

Given the size of the wrecks (respectively, thirty-five meters and twenty-five meters, i.e., one hundred fifteen feet and eighty-two feet), it is quite difficult to fit them into a composition completely, even when using wide-angle lenses. Good photographs can also be obtained by shooting platax batfish *(Platax teira)*, and structures of the wrecks, especially the alcyonarian-encrusted propelled of the overturned wreck. Certainly, the two wrecks are a paradise for the macrophotography.

KUREDDU EXPRESS

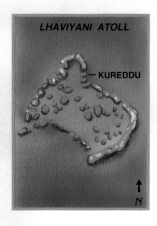

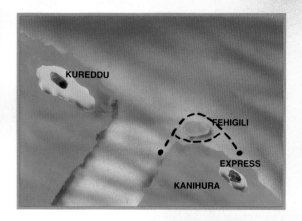

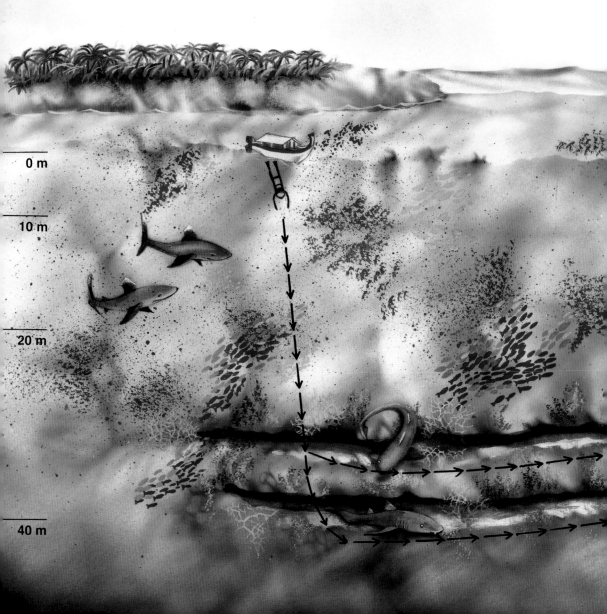

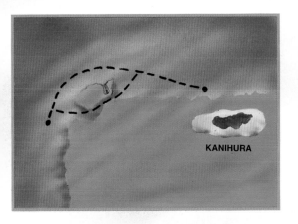

KANIHURA

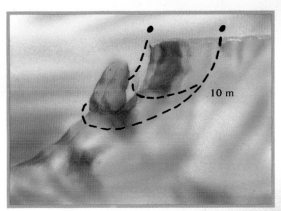

10 m

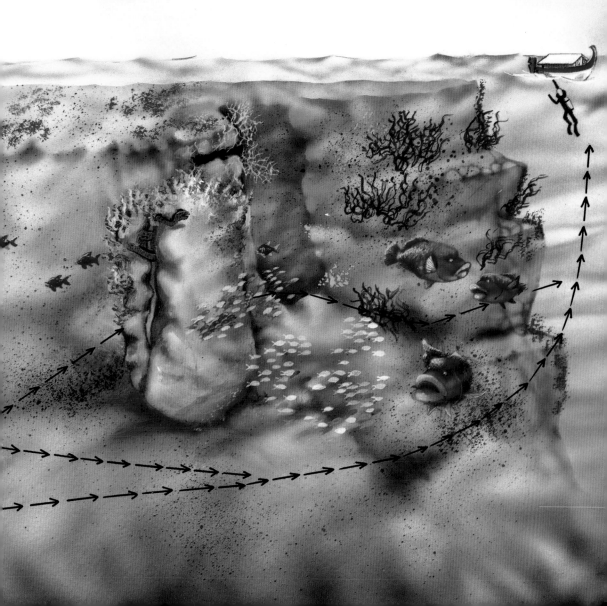

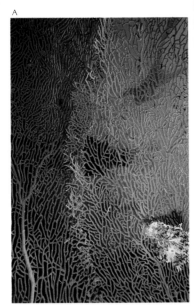

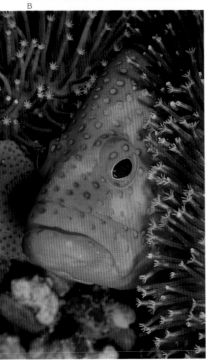

LOCATION

Kureddu Express lies at the extreme north of the Lhaviyani Atoll. It is the southern corner of the channel that separates the islands of Kureddu and Fehigili. At Kureddu stands the only tourist village in the entire atoll of Lhaviyani.

DIVES

This dive should only be made when there is a slight current running inward, or else at the period between tides. The dive begins directly off the small island of Fehigili; then, keeping the wall to one's left, one approaches the corner of the pass, where it is possible to move around the pinnacle, or else stop at the base of same, and look out into the blue waters, awaiting the passage of eagle-rays (Aetobatus narinari), grey reef sharks, and tuna (Thunnus sp.). One ends the dive by allowing oneself to be towed back into the atoll, while remaining close to the left wall of the entrance channel. The use of the scuba tuba helps the boat crew to spot the team.

LIFE FORMS

The outer wall, where the dive usually begins, is characterized, at the depth of thirty to thirty-five meters (one hundred to one hundred fifteen feet), by numerous horizontal cuts that run back into the reef for a distance of two or three meters (six-and-a-half to ten feet), thus forming fissures that abound in reef fish. From the ceilings of these fissures, which are a couple of meters in height, lilac and light-blue alcyonarians hang in dense clumps. The most spectacular part of this dive is an enormous mushroom coral just separated from the wall, right in line with the corner of the pass. Around this squat tower, on the side that overlooks the open ocean, hovers a large school of jacks (Caranx sp.); it is also possible to observe eagle rays (Aetobatus narinari) and grey reef sharks (Carcharhinus amblyrhynchos). The mushroom coral also has a large vertical fissure at the base of which three large morays (Gymnothorax javanicus) who live in the same den poke out their heads. The corridor that separates the mushroom from the wall is characterized by large alcyonarians and imposing formations of black coral, around which swim compact schools of snappers (Lutjanus sp.), sweetlips (Plectorhynchus sp.), goggle eyes (Priacanthus hamrur), creating splendid patches of color.
After entering the pass — which does not have a full-fledged vertical wall, and develops upward by terracing instead — it is possible encounter entire families of humphead wrasses (Cheilinus undulatus) of all sizes.

SAFETY

The name Express says it all about the intensity that current reaches at times in this area; it is therefore necessary for the divemaster — before allowing a group to dive — to enter the water to check the current. Since, in any case, this is a drift dive, one should check to ensure that all of one's utilities are nicely fastened, so as to avoid anything catching in the coral nooks and crannies. It is also important, once one has entered the pass, to stay close to the walls of the pass, so as to have a point of reference.

A - This picture emphasizes the delicate filigree structure of the branch of a sea fan.

B - Hidden amidst the branches of an alcyonarian, a coral grouper (Cephalopholis miniata) waits in ambush for prey.

C - Exceedingly rare blue alcyonarians cover the wall of the reef.

RESPECT FOR THE ENVIRONMENT

A correct balance is important lest one damage the seabed, when doing a drift dive, and when making a halt it is best to do so either on a sandy bottom or upon dead coral.

PHOTOGRAPHY

Given the configuration of the reef and the tranquillity of the schools of territorial fish, one can use all of the wide-angle lenses, such as the 15- and 20-mm.
Excellent photographs can be shot from inside the grottoes toward the exterior, with a view of the alcyonarians that hang from the roof (lighting with the flash turned upward), and a scuba diver swimming in the light-blue depths.

D - A large, solitary carangid (Caranx ignobilis) plies the waters near the coral reef.

E - A dense school of bluestriped snappers (Lutjanus kasmira) swims up along the reef wall, illuminating with golden reflections.

F - A giant moray (Gymnothorax javanicus), surrounded by tiny cleaner shrimp, peers from its den.

G - A saddleback butterflyfish (Chaetodon falcula) displays its distinctive coloring, marked by two large black areas that stand out on its back.

BAA ATOLL - *DIGALIHAA THILA*

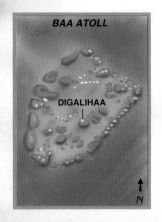

BAA ATOLL

DIGALIHAA

N

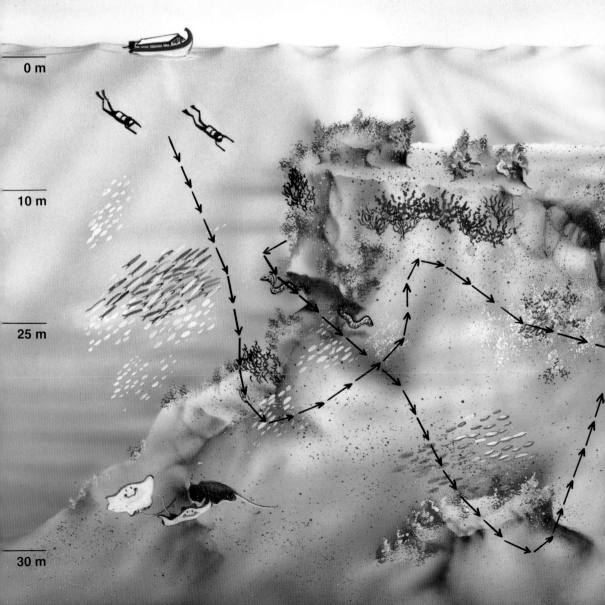

0 m

10 m

25 m

30 m

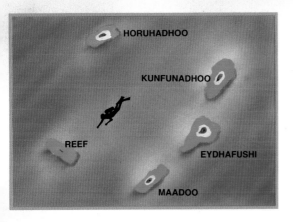

HORUHADHOO

KUNFUNADHOO

REEF

EYDHAFUSHI

MAADOO

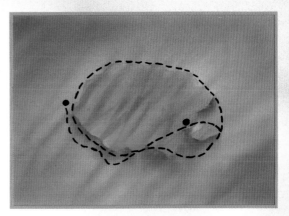

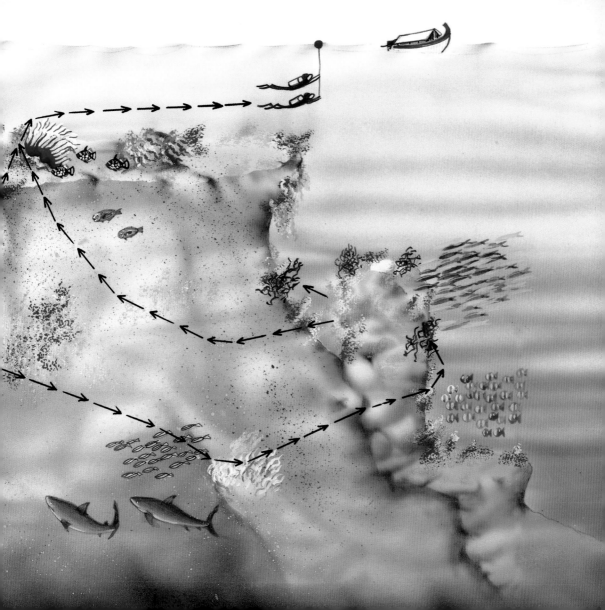

LOCATION

Digalihaa Thila lies in the atoll of Baa. The nearby islands are those of Kunfunadhoo, which was frequented by tourists in the past, and the two islands, Eydhafushi and Maadoo. The highest point on the *thila* lies seven meters (twenty-three feet) beneath the surface of the water, while the overall length is about eighty meters (two hundred sixty feet). At a range of depth from thirty to forty meters (a hundred to a hundred and thirty feet), the ocean floor once again becomes relatively level. Digalihaa is not very heavily frequented by divers. Since there are currently no tourist facilities on the atoll of Baa, it is only possible to go there by safari boats.

DIVES

At Digalihaa, one uses the classical thila diving technique that we have analyzed in some detail in this book. This place, in the presence of strong currents, should only be toured with drift-dives from the open waters. The projections of the reef offer an excellent shelter against even the strongest current. A complete circuit of the coral base, as vast as that base may be, is possible, as long as there is no current and as long as the dive is done under ideal conditions, which is to say, slightly beneath the edges of the reef.

LIFE FORMS

Digalihaa is a paradise for divers because of the enormous range of fish species. This *thila* attracts marine fauna like an oasis in the middle of the ocean. There are impressive schools of jacks *(Caranx sexfasciatus)* that range around the reef. A large school of barracuda *(Sphyraena sp.)* is normally found in the deep blue waters above the edges of the reef, while it is always possible to see a number of large grey reef sharks *(Carcharhinus amblyrhynchos)* when the currents are strong. Aside from these pelagic fish, there is a great mass of other fish, representing the entire range of tropical reef fish. Generally, these fish are rather timid, which should be attributed to the fact that few divers use this site. On the summit

A - A grey reef shark (Carcharhinus amblyrhynchos) is accompanied by a small remora, or sharksucker (Echeneis naucrates) that has fastened itself just under its mouth. The shark's belly presents a number of wounds, probably the "souvenirs" of a recent mating.

B - A scuba diver swims in the midst of a school of elegant fusiliers (Caesio teres), which differ from their close counterparts by the spectacular yellow coloration of their back and their caudal fin.

C - A number of batfish (Platax teira) drift elegantly with the rhythm of the current.

D - An enormous school of bigeye trevallies (Caranx sexfasciatus) swims along the reef walls.

of the reef, one should examine the areas amongst the large coral blocks. In this region, one is likely to find some very large nurse sharks *(Nebrius ferrugineus)*. One coral block on the plateau in particular is entirely covered by a giant sea anemone that is home to hundreds of clown fish *(Amphiprion nigripes)*. This *thila*, especially its summit, teems with a multitude of soft corals, and lastly, there is an authentic forest of black corals near the northwestern scarp. When there is no current at the summit of the *thila*, an enormous school of jacks *(Caranx sexfasciatus)* loiters there, from time to time swirling around in a circle, giving divers a chance to take some photographs from beneath that are truly remarkable. On the north wall, one encounters a group of batfish *(Platax teira)* that we could describe as "albino", since their surface pigmentation is very nearly white: make sure that you use the strobe at low power. In the fissure that divides the shallows from north to south, there are two fairly rare golden-yellow gorgonians.

SAFETY

Starting with the presupposition that on this site one can only dive from safari-boats, some of which even remain above the *thila* by night, there is a detail that cannot be overemphasized: the sharks in this site are not accustomed to the presence of humans, and they still react in an instinctive manner. The writer has experienced the way in which the sharks here fall into a sort of feeding frenzy if, just before the dive, the galley cook were to toss scraps of fish overboard. The result was a number of real or feigned attack against colorful fins and cameras. In situations of this sort, the less experienced divers may easily fall into a panic. Depending on the depth, this place is suited to divers with all levels of experience. Since the higher part of the reef lies at a depth of about seven meters (twenty-three feet), when doing drift-dives, one should make the safety-stop in the open waters. Since the divers will then be dragged away from the *thila* and out into the ocean, it is fundamental to make use of a parachute.

RESPECT FOR THE ENVIRONMENT

Digalihaa is a place in which not many dive. Therefore one does not see here the damage typical of the time in which divers cared less about the environment than they do now. Here too, all the rules and tips concerning the protection of the underwater world still apply. Leave the place where one dives in the same conditions in which one found it — these words should become part of the "honor code" of every scuba diver.

PHOTOGRAPHY

A photographer that knows what he or she is doing could work in this site for an entire week, without running out of ideas. First of all, there is a school of jacks *(Caranx sp.)*, which provides some spectacular visuals. The photographer ought to try to have his or her diving partner or model swim toward the center of the school. The fish will almost certainly begin to swim around the intruder. As a result, the photograph will show a scuba diver in the midst of a huge spiraling crowd of glittering fish. The best lens to use in such a situation would be a wide-angle lens with a from 90 to 160 degrees. The strobe should be set carefully so that the jacks are not overexposed.

E - This sea anemone, which has entirely covered a block of coral, is home to a number of Maldive anemonefish (Amphiprion nigripes), which can be easily recognized by their distinctive orange-yellow coloring, crossed by a white band.

F, H - Numerous multicolored alcyonarians enrich the walls of the reef.

G - The solid surface of the ocean serves as the background for a splendid sea fan.

E

RASDHOO - *MADIVARU KANDU*

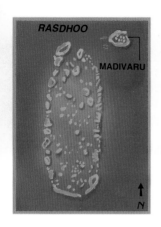

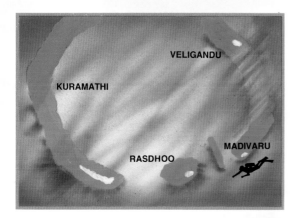

KURAMATHI

VELIGANDU

RASDHOO

MADIVARU

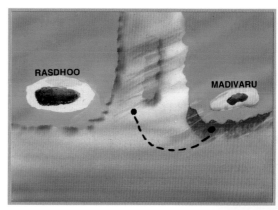

RASDHOO

MADIVARU

LOCATION

This dive lies in the southern part of Rasdhoo, a small atoll to the north of Ari which includes four islands: Rasdhoo, Veligandu, Kuramathi, and Madivaru. In particular, the ledge at the outer edge of the channel that separates Madivaru from Rasdhoo.

DIVES

A classic waiting dive for the purpose of seeing large pelagic fish. One enters the water along the outer reef of the island of Madivaru, and upon reaching the depth of eighteen to twenty meters (fifty-nine to sixty-five feet), one finds oneself on a sandy terrace about thirty meters (one hundred feet) in width. Heading south the diver crosses it widthwise and then arrives at the perfect vantage-point for a view downward into the blue depths. Keeping the wall on the right one reaches the corner of the pass, at a depth of thirty meters (one hundred feet). At this point, the diver makes a halt to observe the passage, and then he allows the current, which is not very strong, to pull him toward the interior.

A - The pectoral fins and broad spinal rays give the turkeyfish (Pterois volitans) a pleasant and delicate appearance that belies its true venomous menace.

B - This scuba diver, shining his light on the alcyonarians that cover the coral wall, highlights their vivid colors.

LIFE FORMS

This is one of the best known places in which to see hammerhead sharks *(Sphyrna lewini).* In all likelihood, the great migrations of these sharks lead them to travel frequently through the channel leading between the atolls of Ari and Rasdhoo. The best moment in the day to see them is, without a doubt, just after dawn, when they swim at accessible depths. In the course of this dive it is always possible to see schools of jacks *(Caranx sp.)* and barracudas *(Sphyraena sp.),* and tunas *(Thunnus sp.)* of quite impressive size. After entering the channel, one finds schools of snappers *(Lutjanus kasmira),* a dense crowd of batfish *(Platax teira),* and the ever-present whitetip reef sharks *(Carcharhinus albimarginatus).*

C - In the channel that separates Madivaru from Rasdhoo it is quite common to encounter small groups of pinnate batfish (Platax teira).

D - A veritable wall of bluestripe snappers (Lutjanus kasmira) swims in procession past the photographer. The tendency of these fish to gather in large schools is in part an attempt to protect themselves from larger predators.

SAFETY

One should pay very close attention to the depth of one's dive. Often schools of hammerhead sharks swim beneath the step of the pass, and when the water is particularly clear, they seem "only a fin-stroke away." In reality, they are far deeper than they look, and are beneath the depths normally attained by sports divers. The understandable enthusiasm of this sort of experience should not lead one to forget the basic rules of safety;

E - Dives in the waters of the Maldives often present certain features, such as encounters with sizable groups of barracudas (Sphyraena sp.) that swim elegantly through the water.

each diver should be the best judge of his or her own technical skills and limitations.

RESPECT FOR THE ENVIRONMENT

When one selects an observation zone in which to make a halt, it is important to pay close attention to the many gorgonians that are found on the walls and on the many tiny terracings of the reef. If there is current, try to avoid clamping on if possible, and always lean only on dead corals which offer a good hold.

PHOTOGRAPHY

The best lenses to use are those for photographing of large schools of fish, such as 20- and 28-millimeter lenses. The strobe should be set at low power because one will be photographing subjects (sharks, barracudas, tunas) of an extremely reflective nature. The best compositions will be those shot upward from beneath, with the silhouettes of the fish seen against the light.

F - Sponges, gorgonians, and alcyonarians transform the seabeds off the islands of the archipelago of the Maldives into a genuine underwater garden, giving a photographer an endless array of interesting views and compositions.

G - Madivaru Kandu is a diving area famous for the sightings of hammerhead sharks (Sphyrna lewini). In order to better observe these "lords of the sea" it is best to dive in the early hours of the morning, when the sharks pass in the shallow waters.

ARI ATOLL - *UKULAS THILA - MANTA POINT*

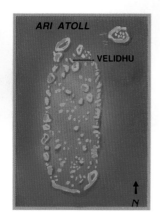

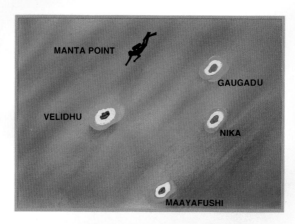

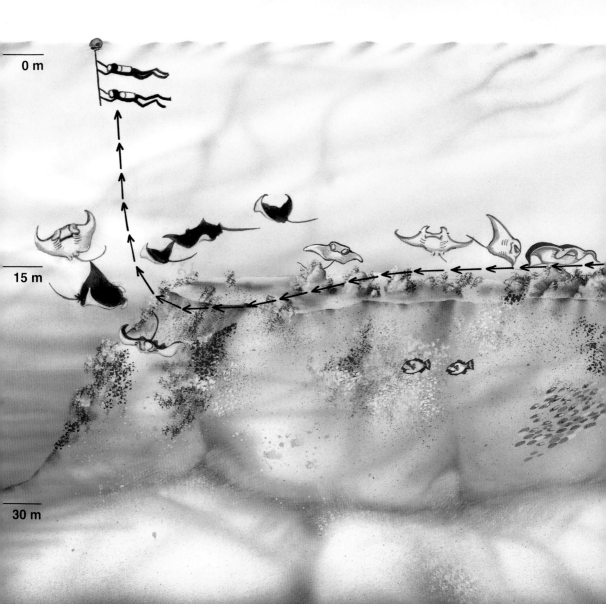

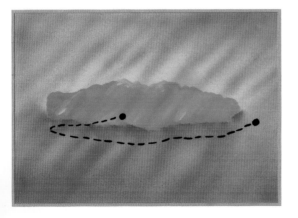

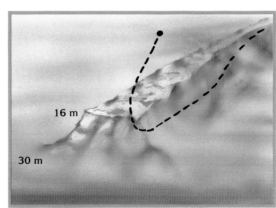

16 m

30 m

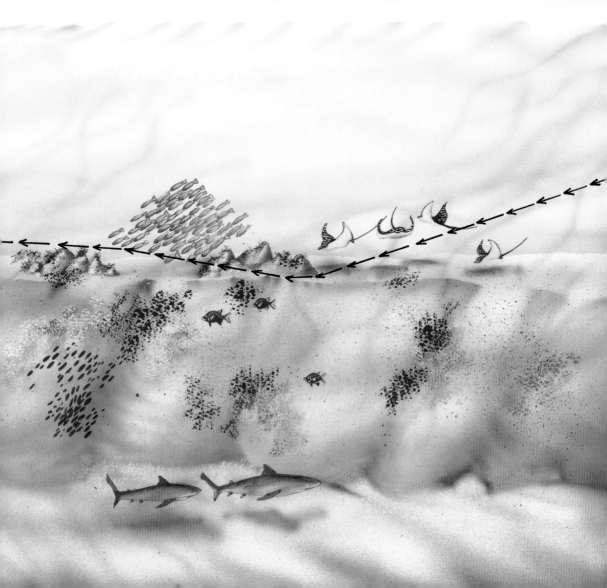

LOCATION

Manta Point lies in the northern section of the channel leading out of the Ari Atoll. Nearby islands are Nika, Gaugadu, and Velidhu. Still further south lies the island of Maayafushi, which lies about twenty kilometers (about twelve miles) from this truly remarkable place. Manta Point is nothing more than a platform which rises at the bottom of the channel from the depth of thirty meters (a hundred feet) to a depth of just sixteen meters (fifty-three feet) beneath the surface.

It is a sort of highland that extends on either side of the channel itself for a distance of two hundred fifty meters (about eight hundred twenty feet), from east to west.

DIVES

Manta Point is a location for advanced divers. Since this site looks out onto the open ocean, in the presence of adverse weather conditions, wave action may be generated such that great diving skill and experience are required. The location of the reef, set crosswise against the channel, is practically ideal for dives that call for the team to drift-dive in from the open ocean with the currents. Above the platform, or when the currents become stronger, one can imitate the way the mantas seek refuge behind projections. The base time increases considerably if one intends to make a halt among the large coral blocks set on the platform; the minimum safety stop of three minutes must in any case be completed in the open ocean.

LIFE FORMS

The main attraction here, of course, are the mantas *(Manta birostris)*, which can regularly be found on the western side of the platform from December until the middle of April. In biological terms, the topography and the location of the *thila* make it an ideal habitat for all the species of fish that live on plankton.

A - A number of bluegreen chromis (Chromis viridis) wend their way through the branches of an acropora. These fish tend to gather in numerous groups, and to colonize specific coral formations, where they find protection and nourishment.

B - Giant mantas (Manta birostris) constitute one of the chief attractions of Ukulas Thila. Adult specimens can grow to a remarkable size, their "wingspans" at times exceeding six meters, or twenty feet.

C - During the daylight hours, it is common to encounter a large school of snappers (Lutjanus kasmira), swimming along the walls of the reef.

D - The dark silhouette of a giant manta (Manta birostris) stands out sharply against the surface of the water. In contrast with legend and popular beliefs, the giant manta is a docile and peaceful creature, which often allows itself to be approached by scuba divers.

E - In this picture, it is possible to observe clearly the way in which mantas feed: they swim in plankton-rich waters and, with the help of their head fins, they channel water that is abundant in microorganisms into their large mouths.

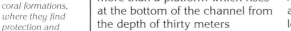

The currents, which intersect at a right angle and cross this platform, sweep the waters and all of the microorganisms that live concentrated in these waters, directly toward the upper edge. The mantas, therefore, need do no more than to hover there with their mouths agape.

There is a great deal more to discover on the *thila*, however. Aside from the bluestriped snappers *(Lutjanus kasmira)* and the eagle rays *(Aetobatus narinari)*, which hover there constantly, on this reef it is possible to observe marine fauna of all sorts, swept here by chance on the currents.

SAFETY

Manta Point lies at the center of a channel which runs north and empties into the open ocean. This fact should always be kept in mind when planning one's dives, especially in terms of the outflow of the currents. All of the precautions listed in this book are particularly applicable at Manta Point. As mentioned above, when the weather is bad, the wave action at the entrance of the channel can be powerful. In order to allow the crew of the boat to find one easily, the parachute should be inflated properly, so that it floats well above the surface.

RESPECT FOR THE ENVIRONMENT

Large coral blocks have established themselves all over the platform. When the currents allow, one should stay at a cautious distance from the top of the reef.

PHOTOGRAPHY

It is difficult to imagine that there are photographers who, on this dive, should choose to equip their cameras with macro lenses. Certainly, everyone will attempt to take a photograph of one, or perhaps even of several manta rays, but it is extremely difficult to determine the depth required to do so, in that the animals'

orientation tends to change from situation to situation.
In order to obtain photographs that are rich in contrast, it is necessary to try to shoot with a super-wide-angle lens from the closest possible distance.
It helps to remember that manta rays tend to be less shy if the photographer swims beneath them, or at the same depth.
For photographs of manta rays and of sharks, as well as of all large fish that can be photographed in open water, one should use a very weak flash. Otherwise, there is the risk of over-exposure, so that the background is very dark and the particles in suspension in the water will appear in the photograph.

E

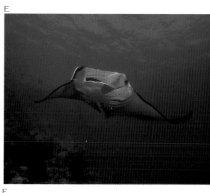

F

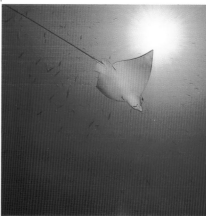

G

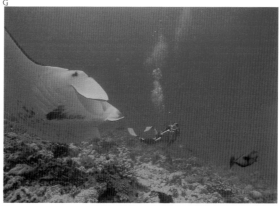

H

F - On the Ukulas Thila it is not uncommon to encounter eagle rays (Aetobatus narinari). These creature, which have tails three times the length of their body, armed with jagged spines, are actually rather timid; to observe them properly, it is recommended to swim beneath them.

G - A scuba diver swims alongside a giant manta (Manta birostris). These creatures have dark dorsal coloring and white bellies with a few dark spots; it is the arrangement of these spots that allows one to distinguish between individuals of the species.

H - The frightful stonefish (Synanceia verrucosa) camouflages itself amidst the coral, so that it looks exactly like a rock; the only features that can be seen are the mouth and the eyes.

MAAYA THILA

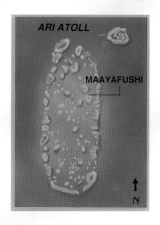

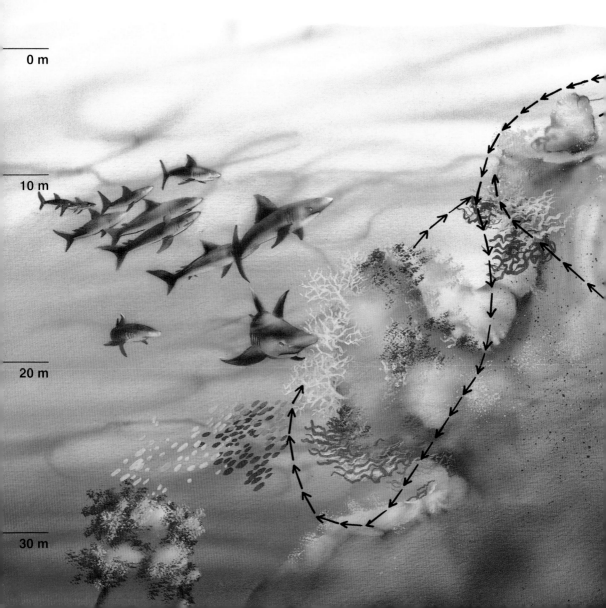

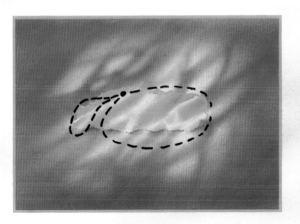

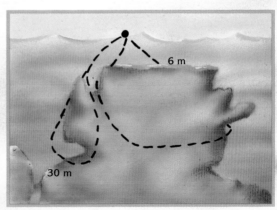

6 m

30 m

LOCATION

Maaya Thila lies within the reef in the northern section of the Ari atoll, to the west of Maayafushi. The size of the *thila* is about fifty meters by thirty meters (about a hundred sixty-five feet by a hundred), while its shallowest point lies about six meters (twenty feet) beneath the surface. The coral base remains exposed to the ocean currents, and is therefore a true paradise of diverse forms of life.

DIVES

The boat can be moored to the *thila* by making use of a permanent mooring set in a special coral block. In the presence of strong currents, one should plan the dive carefully, so that the air is ample for getting out and getting back. As has already been pointed out in the descriptions of other

dives, it is possible to approach this sort of *thila* from the open ocean. What is most important in the practice of this "advanced technique" is to be particularly careful in judging the direction and the speed of the currents. With weak currents, or with no current, one can swim around the *thila* with no difficulty whatsoever. Of course, that is the sort of dive that gives a visitor the best possible impression of this jewel set in the open ocean.

LIFE FORMS

All those who would like to see a an anglerfish *(Antennarius coccineus)* at least once in their lives will be glad to learn that, in a small nook on the northern side, at a depth of twenty meters (sixty-five feet), it is possible to find these ichthyological rarities. The instructor is likely to know the whereabouts of this place. In the nook in question, there are also two large morays *(Gymnothorax javanicus)*, while in the surrounding area it is possible to encounter groups of grey reef sharks *(Carcharhinus amblyrhynchos)*; the groups include up to fifteen individuals. On the eastern side in particular lives a large school of whitetip soldierfish *(Myripristis vittata)*, while the projecting rocks and sheer reef walls are decorated with marvelous soft corals and gorgonians. At the edge of the reef, on the other hand, there are a number of large zebra morays *(Gymnomuraena zebra)* and a large sea turtle. On the western side of the shallows, at a distance from the same of about twenty meters (sixty-five feet) and a depth of about thirty meters (a hundred feet), a large coral formation rises from the seabed. Standing about four meters (thirteen feet) tall, and about ten meters (thirty-three feet) in diameter, this mushroom coral houses a school of bluestriped snappers *(Lutjanus kasmira)*, which form a splendid golden mass in movement: excellent material for close-up photography or great video or film footage. In the corridor between the *thila* and the mushroom coral, one often encounters a sizable school of small barracuda *(Sphyraena sp.)*, swimming along like a silvery cloud. Two large trees of black coral, on the outer wall of the pinnacle, house a great many hawkfish *(Oxycirrhites typus.)*.

SAFETY

To judge from the description shown here, Maaya Thila is an ideal dive for those with any level of experience at all. On certain days and at certain times, of course, the currents can shift and demand more of a scuba diver. A good briefing on techniques of diving and on the fundamental safety equipment required, especially the parachute, is absolutely necessary under such conditions.

RESPECT FOR THE ENVIRONMENT

Compared with other diving sites, Maaya Thila is small and intimate. The life forms, and therefore also the activity of scuba divers, are concentrated in a single site. Here one must carefully observe all the techniques of environmentalist diving described at the beginning of this book. At times, other restrictions still become necessary. When a *thila* like this one is swept by truly powerful currents, one should not be diving. The only protection, in fact, would then be on the side in the lee of the base, but this too would be perilous. The result of such a dive, with disoriented divers battling against the currents, would be the destruction of many coral colonies.

PHOTOGRAPHY

At Maaya Thila all of the photographs imaginable are possible, from macro photographs to shots taken with the super-wide-angle lens. If one is planning to make more than one dive here, then, the photographer should draw up an outline and bring the appropriate equipment for the shots the photographer wishes to take on each dive. Suggested compositions: close-ups of anglerfish, zebra morays atop the reef, and of course the red soldierfish which, seen against the blue backdrop of the water, create a marvelous contrast.

F

G

H

C - In this picture, an enormous, coral sea fan (Gorgonia ventalina) is seen in all its delicacy.

D - When diving at Maaya Thila it is possible to admire a number of splendid alcyonarians that grow on the sheer walls of the reef.

E - Numerous schools of bluestriped snappers (Lutjanus kasmira) form a yellow mass in continuous movement.

F - An incredible array of life forms are found on the coral reefs of the Maldives: from feather stars, waving in time with the ocean currents to small Anthias *(Pseudanthias squamipinnis), to saber squirrelfish (Sargocentron spiniferum), to the oriental grunts (Plectorhynchus orientalis) which peep out among the corals.*

G - This group of small barracudas (Sphyraena sp.) often hovers just off Maaya Thila.

H - The lively red coloring of the soldierfish (Myripristis vittata) creates a pleasant contrast with the deep blue of the endless ocean expanses.

I - In the waters off Maaya Thila many grey reef sharks (Carcharhinus amblyrhynchos) hover and swim.

A - An inquisitive zebra moray (Gymnomuraena zebrata) pokes its head out of its underwater den. These creatures live chiefly upon crabs, and can grow to be as long as a meter-and-a-half (five feet).

B - A giant moray (Gymnothorax javanicus) patiently submits to the work of four cleaner shrimp which, with minute and painstaking labor, eliminate the numerous parasites that have taken up residence in the giant moray's skin.

I

MUSHIMASMINGILI THILA - SHARK THILA

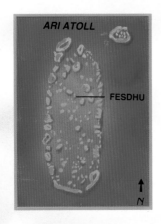

ARI ATOLL

FESDHU

N

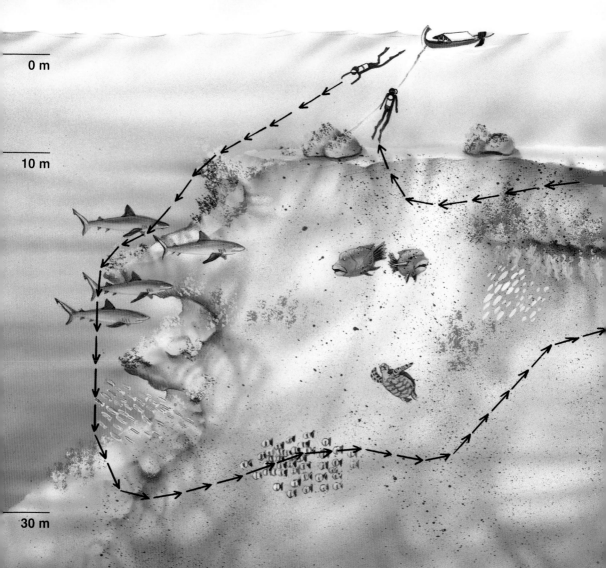

0 m

10 m

30 m

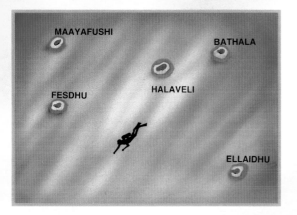

MAAYAFUSHI

BATHALA

FESDHU

HALAVELI

ELLAIDHU

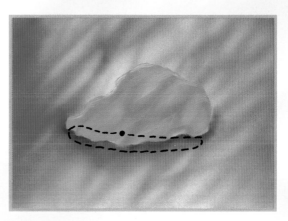

LOCATION

Shark Thila lies within the bounds of the reef itself, but at a considerable distance from the other reefs, in the northern section of the Ari atoll. The closest islands are Fesdhu, Halaveli, Maayafushi, and Ellaidhu. The *thila*, which is about seventy meters (two hundred thirty feet) in diameter, extends in depth to some ten meters (thirty-three feet) beneath the surface.

DIVES

The dives that can be made at Shark Thila are limited to the *thila*, and the boat must be moored at the peak of the reef; very experienced scuba divers however can enter the water off the reef and reach their destination by following the currents. In any event, with *thilas* such as this one, which stand in isolation, it is wise to make use of this technique only if one truly has sufficient experience. In the area around Shark Thila the currents can sweep along with tremendous force, although, in the lee of the base of this formation, calmer waters can always be found.
A general impression of the singular seascape and the enormous variety of fish can be obtained by making a circuit around the *thila*. In order to do this, however, one should await the right moment, when the currents are not running too hard.

LIFE FORMS

This thila is distinguished by an unrivalled abundance of fish, foremost among them sixteen grey reef sharks *(Carcharhinus amblyrhynchos)* who live in the area around the reef, making Shark Thila very famous. Equally noteworthy are the giant schools of

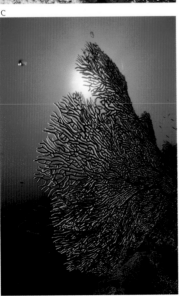

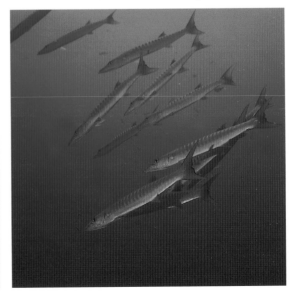

A - A small Anthias (Pseudanthias squamipinnis) with vivid coloring swims along, its mouth agape, in order to feed by filtering the tiny particles of zooplankton in suspension in the water.

B - The upper region of the reef of Mushimasmingili is populated an infinite variety of reef fish, among them the giant moray (Gymnothorax javanicus), which sometimes emerges in pairs from its dens.

C - The delicate branch of a sea fan seems to reach out into the infinite deep, as if to embrace the ocean abyss.

D - The powerful currents around Mushimasmingili attract a number of pelagic fish, including a number of great barracuda (Sphyraena barracuda).

snappers *(Lutjanus kasmira)* that swarm in huge numbers from one reef to another. In the open ocean currents, on the other hand, one often encounters eagle rays *(Aetobatus narinari)*, but the *thila* itself is practically surrounded by all the other species of pelagic fish. Moreover, the area of the reef is enlivened by the entire array of tropical reef fish, noteworthy among them of course morays *(Gymnothorax javanicus)*, which from time to time poke their heads out of their dens, sometimes in pairs. And the dive may be made particularly cheerful by the company of humphead wrasses *(Cheilinus undulatus)*.

SAFETY

There are occasions in which the theoretical and practical principles of hydrodynamics must be kept

E - A large coral grouper (Cephalopholis miniata) ventures close to a scuba diver, showing no fear. This elegant serranid lives near the reef, in grottoes or crannies of all sorts.

F - An antenna turkeyfish (Pterois antennata) rests between a crinoid and a sea cucumber.

G - Perhaps frightened by the arrival of a scuba diver, a number of saber squirrelfish (Sargocentron spiniferum) take shelter in a cranny of the reef.

firmly in mind and observed scrupulously, and this dive is one of those occasions. One must designate a safety stop along the mooring line of the boat, and the scuba diver must refer back to those lines in order to find the point at which he entered the water. It is therefore extremely important to pay close attention to the instructions given by the divemaster. If one should happen to be dragged by the current to some distance from the reef, then the safety stop should be made in open water. The more powerful currents can drag a team of divers hundreds of meters (yards) in just three minutes. Like in any dive in the area around isolated reefs, it is crucial to bring a parachute.

H - The thila of Mushimasmingili is also known by the name of Shark Thila, because of the grey reef sharks (Carcharhinus amblyrhynchos) that swim patiently in the waters off the reef.

I - A solitary hawksbill turtle (Eretmochelys imbricata) seems to glide over the water, near the coral reef.

A

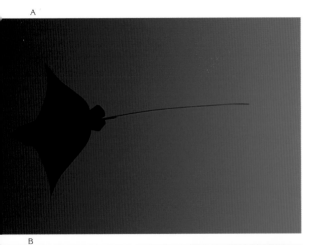

B

C

D - A blackspotted stingray (Taeniura melanospilos) offers itself to the photographer's lens in an unusual angle.

E - Because of its extended snout, the longnose butterflyfish (Forcipiger longirostris) manages to catch the small invertebrates on which it feeds, prying them from the nooks and crannies in which they hide.

F - The soldierfish (Myripristis vittata) enlivens, with its red coloring, the upper section of the reef of Mushimasmingili.

G - The close-up of a multicolored parrotfish (Scaridae) shows the remarkable configuration of its teeth, which join to form a beak composed of four plaques.

H - The open mouth of this coral grouper (Cephalopholis

miniata) might seem frightening, but in reality the fish is patiently waiting for the tiny cleaner shrimp to finish its work.

I - The silvery coloring of a solitary giant trevally (Caranx ignobilis) reflects the sunlight. These fish can grow to remarkable sizes: 1.7 meters (sixty-eight inches) in length and more than fifty kilograms (one hundred ten) in weight.

D

E

A - Spotted eagle rays (Aetobatus narinari) drift hovering along the currents of the open ocean. In this photograph, one can see a splendid specimen, a permanent guest of the thila.

B - The entire group of grey reef sharks (Carcharhinus amblyrhynchos) of Mushimasmingili stages an unsettling whirl of menacing shapes near the reef.

C - A dense school of fusiliers (Caesio sp.) swims in such close formation that the sunlight cannot filter through.

RESPECT FOR THE ENVIRONMENT

If the earliest divers to explore Shark Thila had only behaved with the same respect for the environment that is exercised today, the reef would certainly have a different appearance today. In a place that is swept by abundant currents, such as this, it is especially important to keep at an appropriate distance from the corals. In case of forced halts, there, it is necessary to seek out dead or at least dying reefs.

G

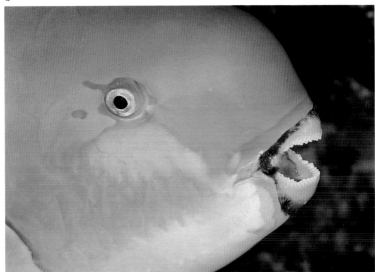

F

PHOTOGRAPHY

In the presence of the appropriate currents, and if the water is sufficiently clear, excellent photographs can be taken of sharks. Some time ago, divers regularly fed the sharks; therefore, probably mindful of those years, the sharks tend to approach divers closely. In order to take a full-frame photograph of a grey reef shark two meters (six and a half feet) in length, the best lenses to use are 24- and 20-millimeter lenses.

The best lenses to use to photograph this remarkable seascape are fisheye lenses. In the higher, shallow portion of the reef, if the currents are not too strong, macro 35-, 50-, and 105-millimeter lenses can be used to make remarkable photographic portraits of the fish.

H

I

HALAVELI - THE WRECK OF THE STINGRAYS

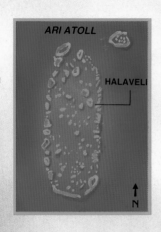

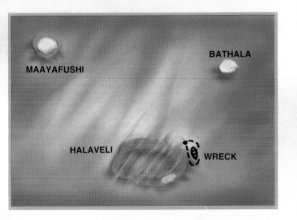

MAAYAFUSHI

BATHALA

HALAVELI · WRECK

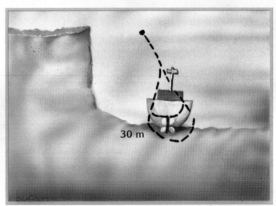

30 m

A

LOCATION

The wreck of the Stingrays lies in the northern section of the Ari Atoll; in particular, on the north-northeast side of the reef surrounding the reef of the island of Halaveli. All that remains of this liner lies at a distance of about thirty meters (a hundred feet) from the actual edge of the reef, on the sandy seabed at a depth of thirty meters (a hundred feet).

HISTORY

This thirty-meter (hundred-foot) liner was sunk in 1991, intentionally, as an attraction for scuba divers.

DIVES

Moor the boat directly on the bowsprit of the wreck, and it thus becomes possible to dive and to return to the surface using the mooring lines as handholds. This site is ideal for divers with a wide variety of levels of expertise, because the deck is just twenty meters (sixty-five feet) beneath the surface, while the superstructure is only seventeen meters (fifty-five feet) deep. Moreover, the currents and the other environmental conditions can be described as being absolutely normal.

B

A - A blackspotted stingray (Taeniura melanospilos), the principal attraction of this dive, and a number of sharksuckers (Echeneis naucrates) allow themselves to be approached by the scuba diver, showing no fear.

C

B - A cloud of glassfish (Pempheris vanicolensis) reflecting a warm and glittering light on the interior of the liner, intentionally sunk with a view to creating a new tourist attraction.

C - Although it was only sunk in 1991, the ship is entirely covered with multicolored alcyonarians and odd coral formations.

LIFE FORMS

Diving in this location offers two truly interesting attractions. First of all, it is possible to encounter an entire group of large blackspotted stingrays *(Taeniura melanospilos),* which swim in a circle around the wreck, displaying not the slightest fear of scuba divers. These fish, quite large, should not however strike fear into the diver, even though their tails are armed with barbs. There are a great many diving sites, scattered all over the world, in which rays of this sort can be touched with the bare hand without the slightest harm ensuing. One must simply be certain to swim along beneath or in the same direction as the rays. Behind them hover a great number of batfish *(Platax teira)*

D - In this aerial view, it is possible to admire the island of Halaveli, which lies at the edge of the broad coral atoll.

D

which show absolutely no fear of divers and seem to be posing for lovely photographs, the light behind them. Around the wreck swim schools of dozens of sharksuckers *(Echeneis naucrates)* which often seize on to airtanks with their sucking disks. Two large morays *(Gymnothorax javanicus)* poke halfway out of a hole in the forward deck.

Near the cabin swim a great many glassfish *(Pempheris vanicolensis)*, which swim in and out of the ship's hatches, creating a spectacular effect of movement. Large silvertip sharks *(Carcharhinus albimarginatus)* can be seen in the area at times, but it is a matter of luck. These predators generally live in deeper waters, and it is quite rare to find them within atolls. Running head-on into one of these denizens of the sea can make a dive near the wreck of the Stingrays an unforgettable experience.

SAFETY

The location and the depth make the wreck of the Stingray a diving site that is virtually problem-free. The habit of some divers of bringing fish down to feed the stingrays, has led these huge harmless animals to lose their natural fear of man.

The largest one on the reef, easily recognizable by its truncated tail, is about two-and-a-half meters (eight feet) in diameter. Now these undersea creatures associate the rushing sound of air bubbles with food, and they leave the seabed and cluster round as soon as divers enter the water.

This behavior can frighten divers, especially in those without much experience in the tropics. Divers are advised to keep their hands and arms away from the mouths of the stingrays, and not to bring food along on the dive. If one were to wish to explore the interior of the ship — and one should plan to do so only if one has sufficient experience and skill — then the best thing is to do so under the supervision of a divemaster. One crucial piece of equipment is a good underwater flashlight.

RESPECT FOR THE ENVIRONMENT

Although a shipwreck is theoretically a dead object, there are many creatures living in and about it. Ships rapidly become artificial reefs, and they should be treated as such. Therefore, refrain from touching the rays, even when these animals become intrusive. Nylon stitching on the palms of the diving gloves can cause abrasions on the delicate epidermis of these creatures, leaving them vulnerable to parasites.

E - With their curious eyes, a number of garden eels (Heteroconger hassi) *seem to stare at the photographer in alarm. These fish, which live in large colonies in sandy areas, tend to hide from divers.*

PHOTOGRAPHY

This wreck is the exact size that allows one to fit most if not all of it into a well-composed photograph, especially if one uses super-wide-angle lenses. The best conditions for taking panoramic photographs of this sort, of course, are those of very clear water, in which case daylight and very weak strobes are sufficient.

F - A scuba diver inspects the wreck, whose structures are already heavily encrusted.

G - A small coral grouper (Cephalopholis miniata) *watches the photographer with a curious and partly frightened gaze.*

KUDA THILA - BROKEN ROCK

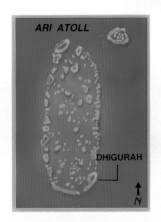

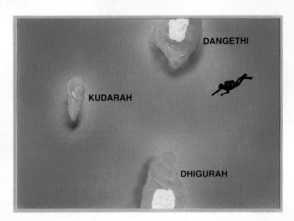

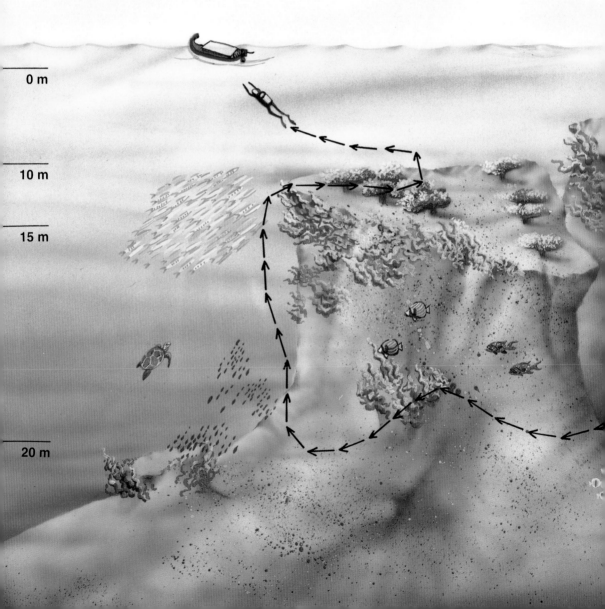

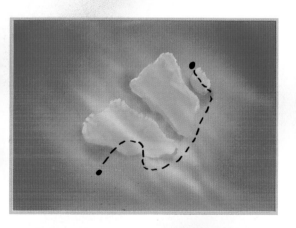

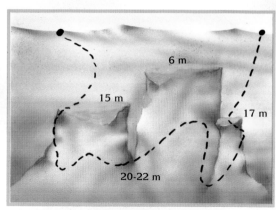

6 m

15 m

17 m

20-22 m

LOCATION

Broken Rock lies in the southernmost corner of the Ari Atoll, on the eastern side. The closest islands are Dangethi to the north and Dhigurah to the south. The *thila*, which seems to have been cleft asunder by a blow from a giant axe, is some seventy meters (two hundred thirty feet) in length, and rises to a depth of some thirteen meters (forty-three feet) beneath

A

B

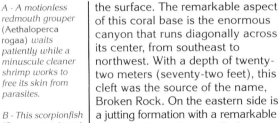

A - A motionless redmouth grouper (Aethaloperca rogaa) waits patiently while a minuscule cleaner shrimp works to free its skin from parasites.

B - This scorpionfish (Scorpaenopsis sp.) gives another example of its remarkable ability to blend in with the seabed.

C - Among the tentacles of a sea anemone, a Clark's clowfish (Amphiprion clarkii) peeks out timidly.

D - As if they were swimming in formation, perfectly synchronized in their movements and their turns, bluestriped snappers (Lutjanus kasmira) are a constant presence along the reef walls.

the surface. The remarkable aspect of this coral base is the enormous canyon that runs diagonally across its center, from southeast to northwest. With a depth of twenty-two meters (seventy-two feet), this cleft was the source of the name, Broken Rock. On the eastern side is a jutting formation with a remarkable shape, and another small plateau, at a depth of seventeen meters.

DIVES

Aside from the considerable depth of the reef top, diving in this site is fairly easy. There are several decisive factors in any decision regarding the techniques to be used on this dive: the currents, which can be very strong at times, but also the level of experience of the participating divers. With weak currents, one can dive directly onto the top of the reef. The most elegant technique, which is also the simplest in the presence of powerful currents, is to dive at some distance from the reef, in the open ocean, and then to swim in to the reef with the current. It is also possible to moor the boat on the reef itself, if it should become necessary to enter and emerge from the water by means of a line.

C

D

E

F

E - Similar to an intricate welter of arms, these sponge formations grow upward toward the ocean surface.

F - The strange coloring of the oriental grunt (Plectorhynchus orientalis) consists of alternating white and black stripes with black dots on a yellow background, and stands out against the dark background of the reef.

G - Often, at the mouths of the underwater tunnels that run through the reef, or of grottoes, enormous sea fans (Gorgonia ventalina) grow, in areas where the fairly powerful currents provide an ideal habitat.

LIFE FORMS

This diving site is embellished by a great many soft corals and by a teeming and varied abundance of fish. Depending on how the current is running, a scuba diver can always encounter different species. Unlike the situation in other sites, the true, permanent inhabitants are few in number.

There is however always the possibility of running into a grey reef shark *(Carcharhinus amblyrhynchos)* or two, or a school of barracuda *(Sphyraena sp.)*. A mixed group of batfish *(Platax teira)* and blue fusiliers *(Caesio lunaris)* are usually guests at Broken Rock, as are the many sea turtles *(Eretmochelys imbricata)*.

The jutting crags on the northeastern side are populated by a great many tiny animals. One can, of course, gain an overall idea of the various animals and corals by swimming all the way around the *thila*, which is eminently possible if the currents are weak.

SAFETY

The plateau of Broken Rock lies at a depth of some thirteen meters (forty-three feet).

This means that, when doing a drift-dive, the safety stop has to be made in the open water with the use of a parachute. If one moors the boat over the summit of the reef, the dive should be planned so as to end near the boat. Particular care should therefore be paid to the direction of the currents and the air supply.

RESPECT FOR THE ENVIRONMENT

As always, when drift-diving one must be careful to keep a greater margin of distance from the corals. The risk of being swept away by currents against a block of coral or against soft corals is, in fact, greater than it would be in calmer waters. A number of parts of the canyon and of the coral base on the northeastern side invite the scuba diver to make a closer examination. But truly tight passages should be avoided, because there is a danger of harming the formations with one's fins or other parts of one's diving equipment.

PHOTOGRAPHY

Broken Rock offers a great many opportunities both with lenses with short depths of field, and with wide-angle lenses. Particularly handsome underwater photography of seascapes can be done near the jutting crags in the northeastern section. In the morning, the interplay of light can be truly remarkable.

G

MULAKU ATOLL- *MULAKU KANDU*

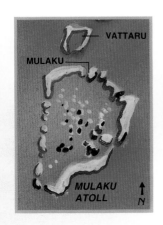

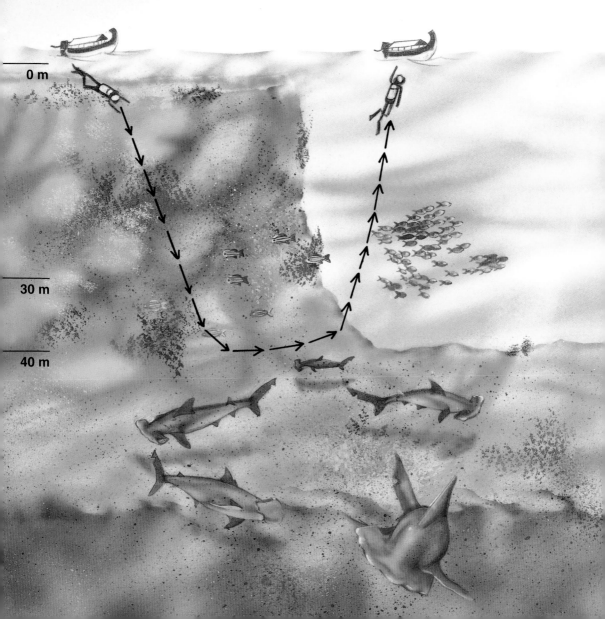

0 m

30 m

40 m

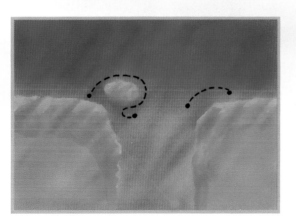

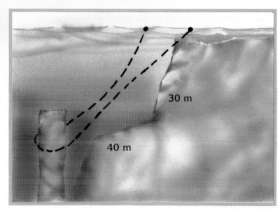

30 m

40 m

A

A - A humphead wrasse (Cheilinus undulatus) poses for the photograph, revealing its massive body structure and the delicate olive coloration.

B - A garishly colored nudibranch rests on a pink alcyonarian, creating an unusual composition.

C, D - The reef of Mulaku Kandu presents countless fissures, nooks, crannies, and passages entirely covered with multicolored soft corals.

B

C

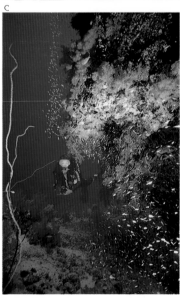

D

LOCATION

Mulaku Kandu lies in the northwestern section of the Mulaku Atoll, and the diving sites lies on the western corner of the pass. In line with the corner, a large block of coral stands detached from the wall, thus forming a pinnacle with a diameter of about ten meters (thirty-three feet), which towers to within twenty meters (sixty-six feet) of the surface. The point at which the coral block and the wall lies at a depth of thirty-five meters (one hundred fifteen feet), while the outer wall drops away into the blue depths. The ledge of the pass lies at the same depth of thirty-five meters (one hundred fifteen feet), with small coral mushrooms.

DIVES

One can dive at Mulaku only by taking a large safariboat, given the considerable distance from any and all tourist villages. In any case, the difficulties of the lengthy trip which is required is amply repaid by the remarkable beauty of the seabeds and by the remarkable encounters with sealife that one tends to make in this area. It is always best to make the dive with a slight current running inward, so that one is not dragged into the atoll too rapidly; one can enter the water directly over the pinnacle, and then swim about it examining the many fissures, crevices, and tunnels that distinguish it, so as to observe the reef fish and soft corals, and then continue downward to the point, at a depth of thirty-five meters (one hundred fifteen feet), where the level seabed enters the pass. Here the diver can pause to admire the blue depths, and then rise at a diagonal along the left-hand wall of the pass. One ends the dive along the upper edge of the reef.

LIFE FORMS

In the entire area surrounding the pinnacle, and upon it, there is an unbelievable concentration of alcyonarians of all shades and hues, which form stupendous matches of vivid color, ranging from red to orange and purple. Above the block of coral and near the mouth of the channel there is regularly a very large of school of jacks *(Caranx sp.)*; a number of barracuda *(Sphyraena sp.)* often swim in and amongst this school. Grey reef sharks *(Carcharhinus amblyrhynchos)* are quite at home here, and they patrol the entrance of the pass at the depth of the terrace that overlooks the dark blue depths. During the first morning dive, one can often observe groups of hammerhead sharks *(Sphyrna lewini)* passing in formation during their migratory travels. It is quite common to encounter eagle rays *(Aetobatus narinari)* when the current is fairly powerful. Along the wall that one follows when rising to the surface, it is possible to encounter sea turtles *(Eretmochelys imbricata)* settled on the reef and every variety of reef fish; these are not at

all timid, and they allow divers to approach them much more closely than is the case elsewhere. One can also rely upon the inevitable visits of some large humphead wrasse *(Cheilinus undulatus)*.

PHOTOGRAPHY

The great chromatic wealth of the soft corals, along with the clear water, make Mulaku a paradise for seascape photography, and one should therefore plan to use 15- and 20-mm lenses. The same lenses can also be used to photograph the school of jacks *(Caranx sp.)*, or to take some close-up shots of small groups of reef fish. With sharks and eagle rays, 20- to 28-millimeter lenses will yield some very good results.

E - The photographer's flash bulb highlights the vivid colors of the alcyonarians that grow on a jutting portion of the reef.

F - Close encounters with dolphins always constitute a unique and exciting thrill. In this picture, one can admire a splendid bottlenose dolphin (Tursiops truncatus).

G - Not far from the reef, aside from the inevitable alcyonarians, there are often feather stars that wave in the flowing current like so many delicate fans.

H - A cleaner shrimp is shown ridding a saber squirrelfish (Sargocentron spiniferum) of parasites. Despite the fact that the shrimp forms part of the fish's usual diet, it ventures in perfect safety, cleaning busily with its tiny claws

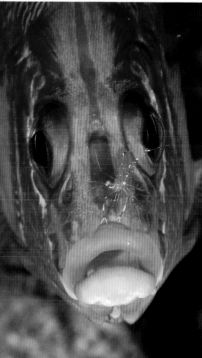

VATTARU - *VATTARU*

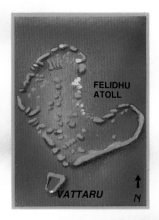

FELIDHU
ATOLL

VATTARU

N

VATTARU

0 m

20 m

40 m

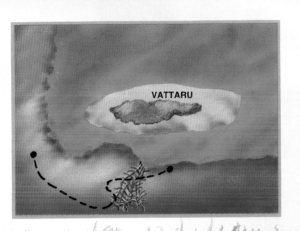

VATTARU

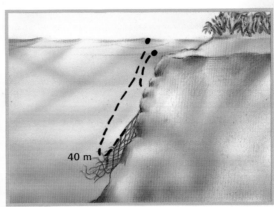

40 m

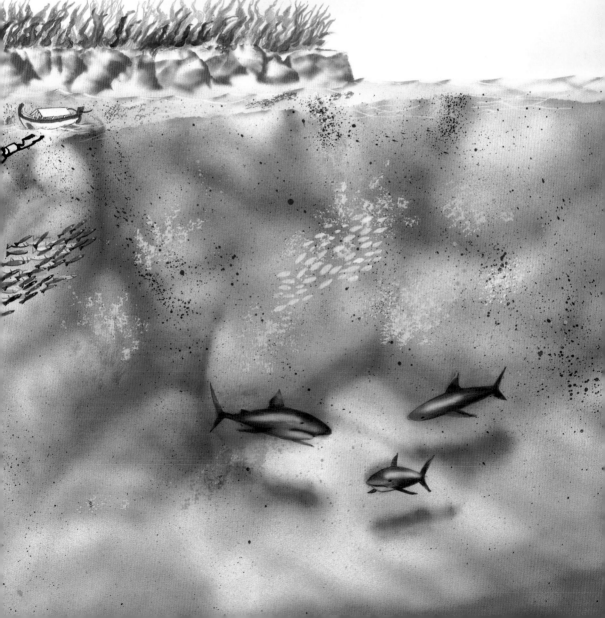

A - A scuba diver prepares to explore a grotto whose entrance is lavishly adorned by multicolored alcyonarians and gorgonians.

B - Following a sea turtle (Eretmochelys imbricata) during a dive often provides excellent opportunities for photographers.

C - Illuminated by the scuba diver's light, a school of glassfish (Parapriacanthus guentheri) glitters like an underwater waterfall.

D - A small group of batfish (Platax teira) swims calmly through the waters off the atoll of Vattaru.

LOCATION

The area of the dive lies along the south wall of Vattaru, a small atoll formed by a large coral ring, interrupted only by a pass; in line with the pass there rises from the ocean a small island, the only one in the atoll to which it gives its name: Vattaru. The exact spot where one dives is in line with a sharp cut toward the shore in the reef, to the north. The reef begins

at a depth of just a few meters (yards), and then plunges down to the ocean depths.

DIVES

This too is a drift dive, although the currents are not particulary powerful in this area: this is a dive that can be made by even the less accomplished divers. It should be planned with the currents running in toward the atoll. One enters the water in line with the point where the reef cuts inshore in the north, forming an area that is protected from the current, and where one

E - Along the walls of the reef, at some thirty-five meters (more than a hundred feet) in depth, one can find tattered remains of a fisherman's net, which is one of the favourite backdrops of photographers who dive in these waters.

F - A clownfish (Amphiprion clarkii) has ventured away from the protection of its sea anemone to better observe the photographer.

can therefore easily reach the proper depth. The first part of the dive is down to a depth of about thirty-five meters (one hundred fifteen feet), to see the tattered remains of a fishing net that dangles from the wall. One then swims up to a depth of twenty meters (sixty-five feet), to view the many small grottoes that can be found at this depth and then, keeping the reef on one's right, one begins to swim upward toward the entrance of the pass, which lies at a depth of eighteen meters (sixty feet). This is quite an unusual pass, in that there is no exterior vertical drop; it simply slopes down into the blue depths, turning into a dazzing expanse of white sand. At this point, the diver should allow him to be carried into the atoll, while swimming around coral mushrooms that give shelter to schools of glassfish and to all the reef fish.

LIFE FORMS

Vattaru is considered by the Maldivians to be one of the areas that most abounds in fish in the entire archipelago; and so, during these dives, one should expect to see dozens and dozens of giant tuna *(Thunnus sp.)*, barracuda *(Sphyraena sp.)*, and pairs of wahoos *(Acanthocybium solandri)*. This last fish is a large vigorous mackerel, fairly difficult to see and one of the most common fish caught by deep-sea fishermen. This is certainly a dive which should be made while looking downward.
At the entrance to a small grotto, not far from the pass, there is a rare anemone with white tentacles.
In line with the bend in the channel, a school of batfish *(Platax teira)* swims along lazily; these fish, perhaps because they are stable residents on the white coral sand, have acquired a light pigmentation, with the almost total cancellation of the dark vertical bands that normally distinguish the species. Whitetip reef sharks *(Carcharhinus albimarginatus)*, their snouts turned into the current, lie lazily on the sandy expanse. In conditions of no current, the channel may be the perfect site in which to watch a number of manta rays *(Manta birostris)* that live here as they feed.

PHOTOGRAPHY

The scrap of net, which has been completely encased by coral concretions, is certainly an ideal subject, worth more than one shot. With 20- and 28-millimeter lenses, it is possible to take shots of tuna and barracuda *(Sphyraena sp.)* in the deep blue waters. For those who like to do close-up photography, white anemones will surely be an obligatory subject, and with a bit of luck, one can capture in a single shot the entire family of clownfish that live, protected, amongst the white tentacles of the anemone. Inside the channel, with wide-angle lenses, one can certainly take pictures of some unusual seascapes.

E

F

G - *A veritable cascade of white alcyonarians descends from the sheer dark wall of the reef.*

G

FELIDHU ATOLL - *RAKEEDHOO*

FELIDHU ATOLL

RAKEEDHOO

N

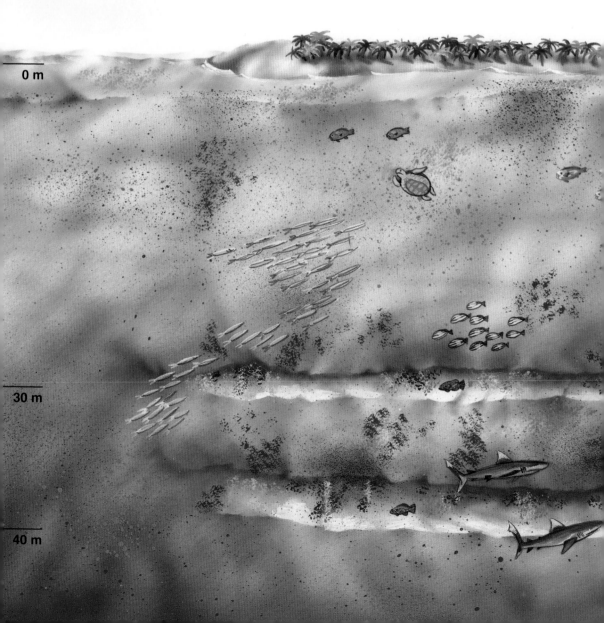

0 m

30 m

40 m

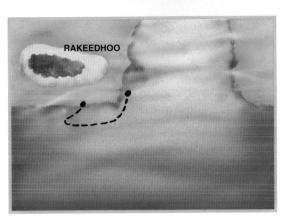

RAKEEDHOO

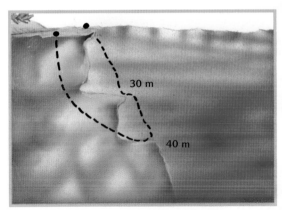

30 m

40 m

A

B

LOCATION

This diving site lies at the southernmost tip of Vattaru. This is the outer wall and the true corner of the western section of the pass, beneath the island of Rakeedhoo. The highest part of the reef comes within two meters (six-and-a-half feet) of the surface, and then drops away sheer into the blue depths, hundreds of meters (yards) below, with broad terracings every twenty meters (sixty-five feet) or so. Given the distance from any large tourist facilities, this dive can only be done with a safariboat.

DIVES

At Rakeedhoo one dives along the outer wall, entering the water at a distance of no more than twenty meters (sixty-five feet) from the corner of the pass. One should observe this precaution carefully because, in this area, when the current enters the atoll, it splits into two segments in this precise spot: one part of the current pours into the atoll through the pass, while the other sweeps around the outer wall, running from east to west. Where the two currents separate, there is a dead-zone known as the "split point," where it is safest to dive. After diving, one should then decide whether to allow oneself to be dragged into the pass or along the outer reef. In both cases, the reef — ranging in depth from three to ten meters, or ten to thirty-three feet — is splendid, with its corals and schools of fish.

A - The silhouette of a scuba diver stands out against the light blue surface of the water while, in the foregroung, a branch of alcyonarian stands out.

B - In this picture, one can detect the rhythmic pulsation of underwater life: hundreds of tiny Anthias (Pseudanthias squamipinnis) swim frenetically around a number of vividly colored soft corals and garishly hued sponges.

C - An enormous sea fan (Gorgonia ventalina) extends its delicately inlaid branches toward the open ocean.

D - During the winter months, it is possible to encounter a number of giant mantas (Manta birostris), that swim alone near the reef of Rakeedho.

C

D

LIFE FORMS

Since this is a dive into an oceanic channel, practically between one atoll and another, large deep-sea fish should be quite at home here. In the open water, it is possible to encounter many different types of shark: from common whitetip reef sharks *(Carcharhinus albimarginatus)* to grey reef sharks *(Carcharhinus amblyrhynchos)*; in the earliest hours of the day, sizeable mako

sharks *(Isurus oxyrinchus)* have been seen in the early morning hours and, near the ledge of the pass, it is possible to distinguish the unmistakable silhouettes of hammerhead sharks *(Sphyrna lewini)* in the deep blue waters. In the corner of the channel an enormous school of bigeye trevallies *(Caranx sexfasciatus)* are found permanently; with their snouts pointing into the current, they form a genuine wall of silver. Beneath these trevallies there is generally a small group of about twenty barracuda *(Sphyraena sp.),* they too waiting motionless for the current to bring them some prey in difficulties. The wall overlooking the open sea, or southward, is distinguished by huge horizontal fissures, which form full-fledged grottoes from the ceilings of which hang bunches of light-blue alcyonarians, while on the floors of these grottoes there are gorgonian fans and "trees" of black coral. One of these grottoes, at a depth of forty-five meters, or about one hundred fifty feet, offers shelter to a grouper that has grown to be two meters (six-and-a-half feet); often this grouper can be seen swimming in the depths with its escort of yellow and black pilot fish moving just before it: this is truly an unforgettable encounter. If one chooses to end the dive along the outer wall of the atoll, one will encounter large concentrations of blue fusiliers *(Caesio lunaris)* and a great variety of reef fish.
In the winter, the occasional large manta ray *(Manta birostris)* swims against the current.

PHOTOGRAPHY

This is a classic dive in which one would require two camera bodies with two different lenses: the first with a 28-mm lens to photograph sharks in the blue water or other deep-sea fish; the second body should have a 15-mm wide-angle lens, for shots in the mixed light inside the grottoes, and in order to photograph the school of trevally which remains almost motionless, and which, with a bit of technique, one can get close enough to touch.

E

E - At sunset, the feather stars extend their soft feathery arms in search for food. By day, on the other hand, in order to protect themselves from predators, they hide by folding themselves into the nooks and crannies of the reef.

F

G

F - A spotted burrfish (Arothron nigropunctatus), perhaps made curious by the presence of the photographer, peeks out of its den. This fish never ventures far from the reef, where it finds protection.

G - These formations of organ pipe coral (Tubastera sp.) are reminiscent of a spectacular explosion of fireworks.

H - These carangids (Caranx sexfasciatus) which swim through the waters of Rakeedhoo at times form an impenetrable wall of glittering silver.

H

FOTHTHEYO

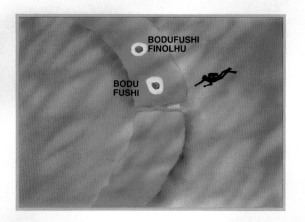

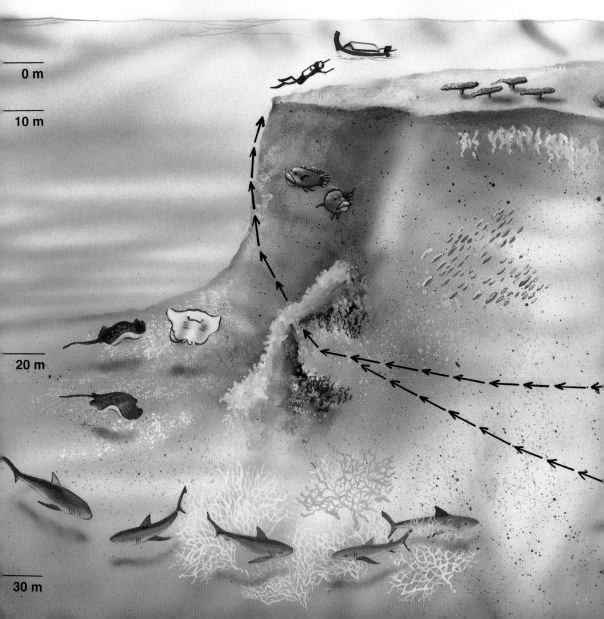

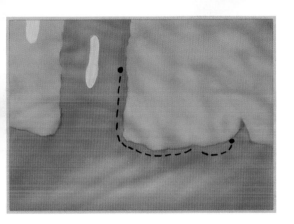

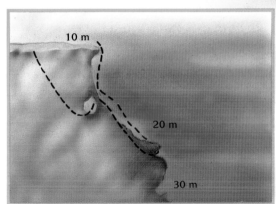

10 m

20 m

30 m

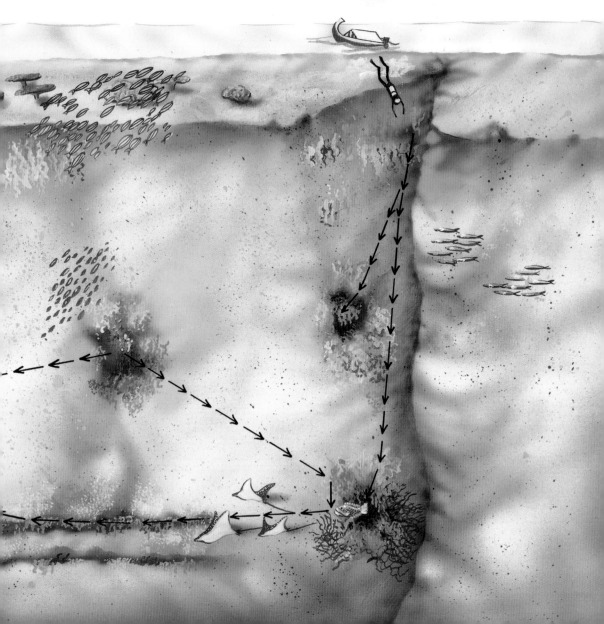

LOCATION

Foththeyo is located on the eastern side of the Felidu Atoll, outside of the reef. The closest islands are Bodufushi and Bodufushi Finolhu. The diving site, which lies outside of the reef, at the entrance of the channel which divides the reef in half, is truly spectacular, in part because of the *thila* which looms up in the channel itself, jutting up to within ten meters (thirty-three feet) beneath the surface of the water, and in part because of the sheer cliff wall before it, which overlooks the open ocean. At depths ranging from twenty-five to fifty meters (eighty-two to one hundred sixty-four feet) there are series of caves with through arches, covered with large formations of white and yellow alcyonarians. At a depth of forty meters, or one

A - A scuba diver shines a light into a cranny in the reef wall, from which countless alcyonarians dangle; in the foreground, one can see a magnificent sea fan (Gorgonia ventalina)

B - Diving at Foththeyo provides a spectacular view, unlike any others: a veritable cascade of white and yellow alcyonarians is the most remarkable feature of this coral reef.

hundred thirty feet, there is a natural through arch, with a span of about twenty meters, or sixty-five feet, at the bottom of which grow many coral sea whips, which float sinuously with the rhythms of the ocean currents. Near the arch, a sort of coral roof juts out toward the ocean waters, and nearby a large schools of jacks is often found. From time to time one can also spot an enormous grouper, which weighs at least two hundred kilograms: imposing it sails past, surrounded by the inevitable entourage of pilot fish.

C - A coral grouper (Cephalopholis miniata) ventures menacingly close to a school of slender sweepers (Parapriacanthus guentheri).

D - At the mouth of an undersea grotto, a great variety of life forms create a harmonious palette of brilliant colors.

DIVES

Foththeyo is considered to be one of the finest sites for diving in all the Maldives, but it is advisable only for those who are already at an advanced level and who possess extensive experience with currents of all sorts. It is in any case a drift dive, which means the dive is possible only when the currents are flowing inward. The diver usually begins at the fissure in the reef, and swims down to a depth of thirty-six meters (about one hundred twenty feet), through a tunnel at the bottom of which grow a great number of red and white whip corals. From the ceiling dangle blue and white alcyonarians, and at the exit there

is an enormous tree of black coral. Otherwise one can enter the grotto with two exits at a depth of twenty-seven meters (about ninety feet), which is also home to an enormous grouper (about two meters, or six-and-a-half feet, long), and then, after emerging from the other side, one continues along at the same depth until, at twenty-five meters (eighty-two feet), one reaches the natural arch that offers a unique spectacle, as it is entirely covered yellow, white, and orange alcyonarians. Then one swims upward a few meters (yards), reaching the recess that corresponds to the entrance to the channel. After swimming into the channel,

E - From the sheer wall of the reef extend huge branches of red fire coral.

F - This picture shows another of the remarkable seascapes that are regularly encountered when diving at Foththeyo.

G - A fairly rare species in the archipelago of the Maldives, red fire corals grow in areas where the rays of the sun cannot penetrate, and it is therefore possible to observe them only at great depths.

H - A small school of oriental grunts (Plectorhynchus orientalis), accompanied by tiny orange Anthias *(Pseudanthias squamipinnis), forms an elegant procession over the coral reef.*

I - Delicately hued alcyonarians and the inevitable Anthias *(Pseudanthias squamipinnis) surround a saber squirrelfish (Sargocentron spiniferum).*

A - In the waters of Foththeyo, where the pass heads out for the open sea, the scuba divers are greeted by a remarkable sight: hundreds of white, yellow, and orange alcyonarians completely cover the sheer walls of the reef.

B - The white tentacles of the polyps of a gorgonian are reminiscent of an image of a tree covered with blooming flowers.

one crosses a sandy area where a great many whitetip sharks (Carcharhinus albimarginatus) lie on the seabed, snouts pointing into the current. One swims up along the ridge of the *thila* which splits the channel in two and juts up to within ten to twelve meters (thirty-three to forty feet) beneath the surface. Reaching the end of the shallows, one swims through the channel in the middle of the water, hugging the right wall, and the dive is complete when one reaches the cliff where, at a depth of eight or nine meters (twenty-six to thirty feet), one can find a number of

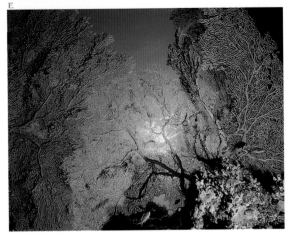

lobsters (Palinurus sp.). Fastened onto the cliff wall, just beneath the entrance to the pass, in the open ocean, are a great many gorgonians with fans of two to three meters (six to ten feet) in diameter.

LIFE FORMS

As we have already pointed out, the entire cliff wall near the exit of the channel teems with soft corals, while in the deeper waters one regularly encounters grey reef sharks (Carcharhinus amblyrhynchos), whitetip reef sharks (Carcharhinus albimarginatus), and a school of eagle rays (Aetobatus narinari). Across the sandy bottom cruise huge stingrays (Taeniura melanospilos), often accompanied by sea turtles (Eretmochelys imbricata). At the top of the *thila* grow large table corals, while fire corals abound in the area around the sandy seabed. Along the length of the *thila* a great many humphead wrasses (Cheilinus

C - The pointed snout and the large menacing eye are outward signs of the aggressive personality of the saber squirrelfish (Sargocentron spiniferum).

D - A scuba diver stops to admire the remarkable masterpiece that nature has created along the walls of the reef of Foththeyo.

E - In this lovely picture, the rays of the sun heighten the delicate beauty of the branches of a sea fan.

116

F

G

H

F - *Splendid huge white alcyonarians seem to emanate light in the underwater gloom of Foththeyo.*

G - *This close-up of a turkeyfish (Pterois volitans) reveals the remarkable flattened structure of the fish's body.*

H - *A hermit-crab reveals itself to the photographer, ready to duck into the seashell that it has selected as a permanent home.*

I - *The lobster is one more element of life and movement on the seabeds and walls of the reef.*

undulatus) live. And a large school of sweetlips *(Plectorhynchus orientalis)* chooses to remain on the reef, practically always near the same corals.

SAFETY

An important safety consideration while diving in the channels is to pay close attention to the currents. The teams that cross the *thilas*, or channel walls, move toward the interior of the atoll, following the in-flowing current, have better control than those that enter the water at some distance from the reef. In any case, each team should bring a parachute. If, on the other hand, one enters the channel from the open ocean, which is to say, from deep water, one must pay special attention not to exceed depth limits.

RESPECT FOR THE ENVIRONMENT

Penetrating into the grottoes and underwater caverns of the sheer cliff wall is an irresistible challenge to scuba divers. The soft corals that stand out against the blue blackground of the ocean depths are certainly spectacular, to photograph or to film. And all of this can be done without even grazing the coral formations, as long as one makes proper use of one's flippers.

PHOTOGRAPHY

The underwater world of Foththeyo is particularly appropriate for the use of wide-angle lenses.
With such focal lenghts it is possible to photograph everything, beginning with the grottoes filled with soft corals and schools of fish.

I

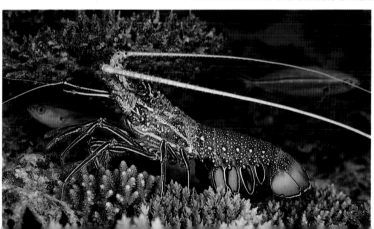

SOUTH-MALE ATOLL - *VAAGALI FARU*

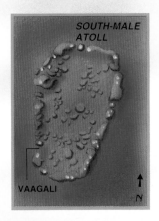

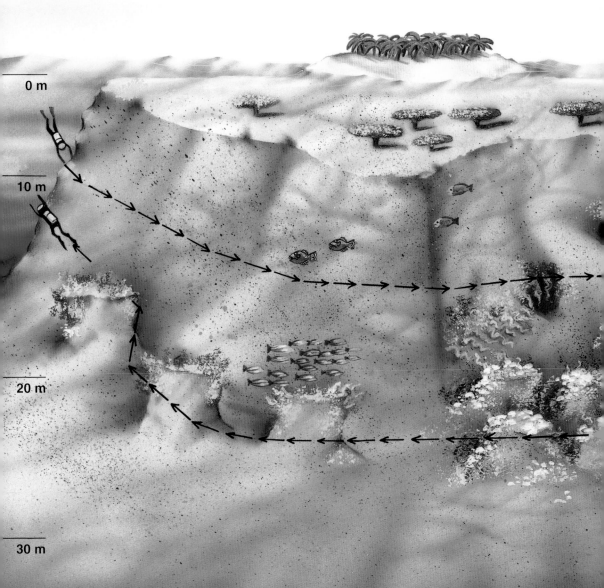

0 m

10 m

20 m

30 m

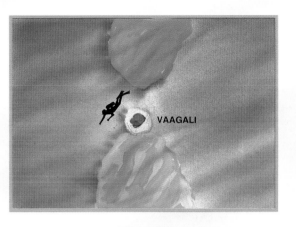

VAAGALI

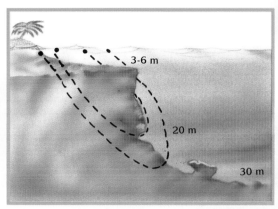

3-6 m

20 m

30 m

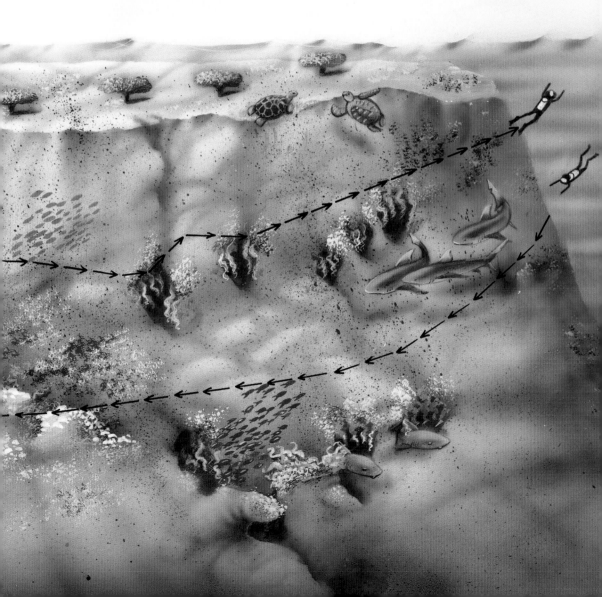

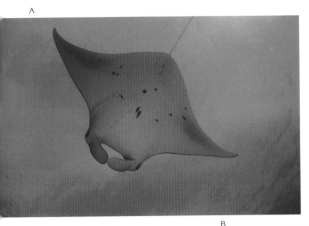

A

LOCATION

Vaagali Faru lies on the western side of the South-Male Atoll, on the exterior of the reef. The nearby islands are Vaagali, also known as "chicken island," and, to the south, Rannalhi. The diving side is the slope of a coral base structure upon which stands the island of Vaagali. The slope begins at a depth of about three meters (ten feet), and then drops away at a relatively steep angle until the outer edge of the reef, at a depth

B

A - The giant manta (Manta birostris) has also been called the devilfish, because of the headfins that resemble two horns and the entirely black dorsal coloring.

B - A small group of slender sweepers (Parapriacanthus guentheri) darts rapidly among the coral formations, bringing glittering light to the gloomy depths.

C - The glint of the photographer's flash highlights the brilliant silvery coloring and the slender outline of a number of carangids (Caranx sexfasciatus) swimming in the night.

D - A giant manta (Manta birostris) rises from the ocean depths toward the light of the sun.

C

of about thirty meters (about a hundred feet). The diving site is quite heterogeneous. From the sandy bed of the channel, which is relatively flat and scattered with large coral blocks, one passes through an area that abounds in grottoes, and finally to the edge of the outer reef.

DIVES

In this spot, only drift-dives are done. When the current is running outward from the atoll, a dive in the canal should begin to the east of the island of Vaagali. One will then emerge on the outer, western side of the reef. When the currents are running inward, one will instead begin from the outer reef, skirting the reef of Vaagali, first to the north and then to the east. Lastly, the dive should end in the so-called "sandy basin" on the interior of the atoll.

LIFE FORMS

There are large soldierfish *(Myripristis sp.)* living in a grotto located at a depth of precisely twenty-four meters (seventy-nine

D

feet), at the outer corner of the reef. Here, one can also site large numbers of whitetip reef sharks *(Carcharhinus albimarginatus)*. In the plankton-rich waters, manta rays *(Manta birostris)* cruise. This part of the reef is also an ideal site in which to surprise a sea turtle *(Eretmochelys imbricata)* or two. On the interior of the channel, in the area around a grotto that ranges from depths of seven to twelve meters (twenty-three to forty feet), there is a large school of fusiliers *(Caesio sp.)*. Depending upon the current, but especially when the current is running in toward the atoll, those who dive in this site can always count on having a big surprise.

SAFETY

In the presence of powerful currents, this site is off-limits to all but those divers who have drift-dive experience. When the currents are weaker, on the other hand, this site is ideal for divers of all sorts, since the edges of the reef lie at depths ranging from three to eight meters (ten to twenty-six feet). When the currents are running outwards, which is to say, when they tend to drag the scuba diver toward the open water, or else dive with the assistance of a parachute. If the current is exceptionally powerful, it is extremely important to swim along very near the reef, especially on the outside corner; otherwise there is the danger of being towed out into the open ocean.

RESPECT FOR THE ENVIRONMENT

Of course, the many grottoes are inviting, but while exploring them, scuba divers should be particularly careful not to damage coral formations with their flippers.
As we have said elsewhere, in the presence of powerful outward currents, it is of great importance to avoid straying from the reef, especially in the area around its southern outer edge. Despite this precaution, one should be exceedingly careful about damaging the coral branches.

PHOTOGRAPHY

From inside the grotto, which descends obliquely toward the sea bed, situated as it is on the wall of the channel, at a depth of ten meters (thirty-three feet), it is possible to take pictures of scuba divers and schools of fish framed by the silhouette of the cavern, against the light-blue background of the ocean water. In the area with the sandy bed, the photographer can rely on truly excellent lighting thanks to the reflection. The large coral blocks are an excellent setting for any type of underwater lens.
With the currents running inward, it would be wise to bring two cameras with one. Outside of the reef and in the channel, one would thus use a wide-angle and a normal lens, while emerging, in the calm waters of the lagoon, one could make macro photographs.

E - Menacingly, a grey reef shark (Carcharhinus amblyrhynchos) prepares to whirl about directly in front of the photographer.

F - Accompanied by the inevitable cleaner shrimp, a yellowmargin moray (Gymnothorax flavimarginatus) makes a fierce display of its bristling teeth.

G - In a typical hunting formation, a number of turkeyfish (Pterois volitans) swim, their fins spread, in search of prey.

GURAIDHOO CORNER

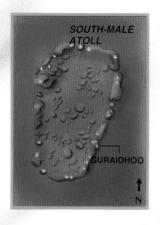

SOUTH-MALE ATOLL

GURAIDHOO

N

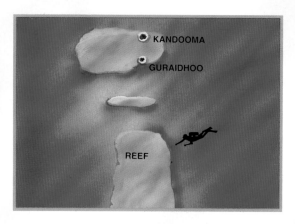

KANDOOMA

GURAIDHOO

REEF

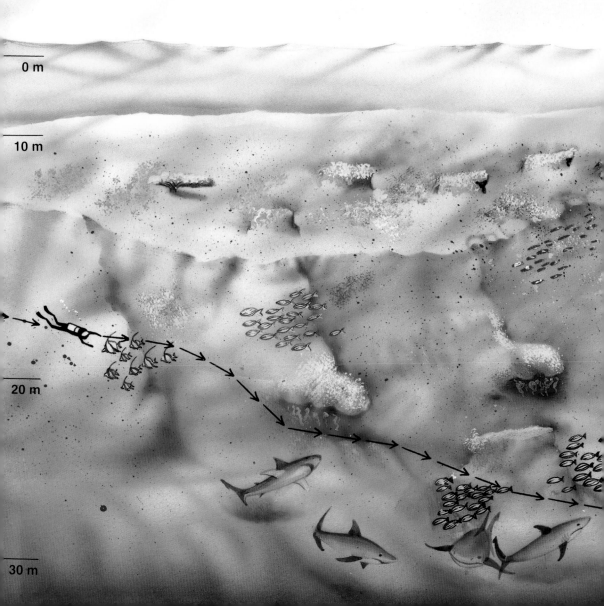

0 m

10 m

20 m

30 m

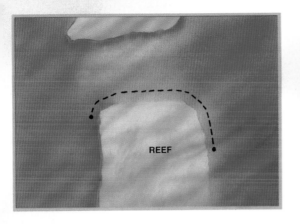

REEF

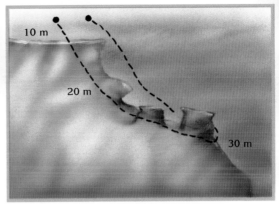

10 m

20 m

30 m

A

LOCATION

This site lies on the east side of the South-Male Atoll, outside of the reef. To be more exact, this is the southern edge of the channel mouth. Nearby islands are Losfushi, Guraidhoo, and Kandooma. The reef top drops from ten meters (thirty-three feet) to thirty meters (a hundred feet) and more; there are grottoes and projections just about everywhere. The edges of the channel drop down to a depth of thirty meters (a hundred feet). Large isolated coral blocks grow, from the scarp of the reef upward.

DIVES

At Guraidhoo Corner only drift dives are possible. It is therefore necessary to be quite an

On the edges of the channel, which is to say, at depths ranging from twenty-five to thirty meters (eighty to a hundred feet), the best chances are that one will be able to observe a great many grey reef sharks (*Carcharhinus amblyrhynchos*) and the local school of eagle rays (*Aetobatus narinari*). The latter tend to swim in the open ocean, at a considerable distance from the seabed. In this same spot, large hammerhead sharks (*Sphyrna lewini*), whale sharks (*Rincodon typus*) and sailfish (*Istiophorus platypterus*) have been sighted frequently. Guraidhoo Corner is also home to large schools of oriental sweetlips (*Plectorhyncus orientalis*), bannerfish

A - A group of spotted eagle rays (Aetobatus narinari) swims in compact formation at the edge of the pass of Guraidhoo Corner.

B - At times, in deep waters, it is possible to encounter elegant specimens of the hammerhead shark (Sphyrna lewini), easily recognized by the unmistakable silhouette of its head.

C - A painted grunt (Diagramma pictum) swims past a majestic gorgonian, surrounded by orange Anthias (Pseudanthias squamipinnis).

B

C

experienced diver on this reef; all the more so because there are powerful vertical currents all around the site at certain hours of the day. The direction of the principal horizontal current is toward the interior of the atoll. At the edge of the channel, which is also the deepest point, one comes drifting along the reef. The dive comes to an end along the wall of the channel or at the edge of the reef.

LIFE FORMS

Because of its location outside of the reef, and because of the water movements and the topography, this place is destined to be the home of larger fish.

(*Heniochus diphreutes*), and large black-and-white striped snappers (*Macolor niger*). And of course the large and friendly humphead wrasses (*Cheilinus undulatus*) are ever-present.

RESPECT FOR THE ENVIRONMENT

While skirting the reef, especially at the beginning, it is fairly easy to maintain an adequate distance from the coral. Greater attention is required when moving away from the edges of the reef. Indeed the reef, which presents fewer and fewer jagged edges, is literally covered with blocks of coral of considerable length and the countless branches of acropora.

PHOTOGRAPHY

The photographer should prepare in advance to take photographs against the light of a school of fish, and a school of eagle rays. The focal lengths, from 20- to 15-millimeters, are perfect for this purpose. Suggested composition: In the presence of clear waters and moderate currents, one should attempt to move out to the open water, beneath the school of eagle rays.

These animals, shot in sharp relief against the light, will make for a rare and spectacular photograph.

D - A sea fan (Gorgonia ventalina) *growing parallel to the reef, offers a solid perch for many sea lilies.*

E - *The powerful currents have assisted the development and growth of broad branches of the gorgonians.*

F - *The waters of Guraidhoo Corner are home to a great many species of reef fish that, with their garish coloring, provide interesting material for the photographer. This photograph shows a number of oriental grunts* (Plectorhynchus orientalis).

G - *A grey reef shark* (Carcharhinus amblyrhynchos) *appears in all its ferocity, in this close-up.*

H - *A yellow "cloud" of bluestriped snappers* (Lutjanus kasmira) *illuminates the ocean depths.*

MIARU FARU - SHARK POINT

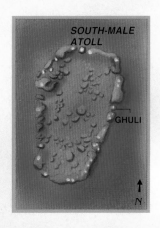

SOUTH-MALE ATOLL

GHULI

N

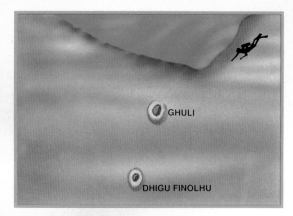

GHULI

DHIGU FINOLHU

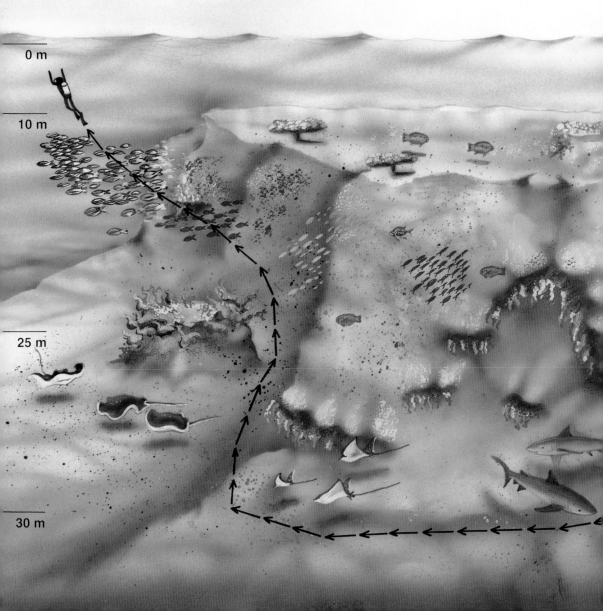

0 m

10 m

25 m

30 m

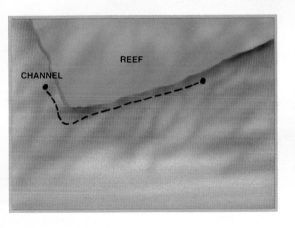

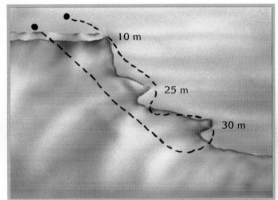

LOCATION

Shark Point lies on the east side of the South-Male Atoll, outside of the reef. The nearby islands are Ghuli and Dhigu Finolhu.
This place is located at the northernmost extremity of the channel, and it is possible to do drift dives here following the incoming current. The surface of the outer reef lies ten meters (thirty-three feet) beneath the surface of the water, and then plunges downward at an angle of 45 degrees. At a depth of twenty-five meters (eighty-two feet), there are a number of underwater grottoes, and the edge of the reef is a sheer wall, especially at the far end of the channel.

DIVES

Shark Point lends itself to drift dives, starting outside the reef and ending inside the channel.
The speed of the current determines the distance and depth from the mouth of the channel at which the teams should be lowered into the water. Lest they be dragged over the top of the reef, it is important from the

D - The rich waters of the archipelago of the Maldives allow a vast array of remarkable and improbable formations of coral to develop and flourish.

A - In a grotto at a depth of twenty-five meters (eighty-two feet) hover a pair of leaf fish (Taenianotus triacanthus). *These exceedingly rare fish present a variable coloring and a fairly well developed dorsal fin.*

B - The silhouettes of three batfish (Platax teira) *stand out sharply against the endless blue expanse of the ocean.*

C - A blackspotted stingray (Taeniura melanospilos) *accompanies the scuba diver during a swim along the sandy seabed.*

beginning that the teams maintain an adequate distance from the wall of the reef itself. At the ends of the channel, the currents can run very strong, but the scuba divers can make use of this condition to drift to the interior of the atoll without exerting much energy. One can dive into this place only if one is an advanced diver, and if one has a great deal of experience of underwater currents.

LIFE FORMS

As the name of the place suggests, it is possible to encounter and observe sharks here; they swim to and fro at the end of the channel, where the currents are strongest. Grey reef sharks *(Carcharhinus amblyrhynchos)* and whitetip reef sharks *(Carcharhinus albimarginatus)* are those most likely to approach scuba divers. But there is more to this place than just sharks and eagle rays *(Aetobatus narinari)*, which are as common and as easy to find, here one can also find yellowish-brown leaf-fish *(Taenianotus triacanthus)*, hidden in a grotto at a depth of twenty-five meters (eighty-two feet). Since these animals are quite difficult to lure out, it is best to rely upon your dive guide.

SAFETY

Techniques and rules for diving in the presence of currents should also be observed at Shark Point. When drifting to the outer edges of the reef, the danger exists that one might be dragged over the reef. If, instead, one swims at about twenty meters (sixty-five feet) of depth, keeping an adequate distance from the scarp, that will not happen. On the edge proper of the reef, the currents become stronger. Those who dive must be well aware that they are thirty meters (a hundred feet) underwater, and therefore one's legs will receive a great deal of exercise. Therefore, one must keep a close eye on one's air supply.

RESPECT FOR THE ENVIRONMENT

When diving in the presence of currents, there is always the imminent danger of harming the

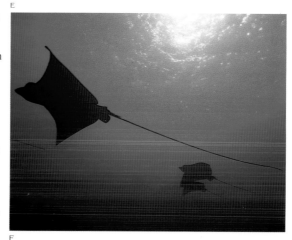

E

F

coral. While drifting along the reef, it is quite simple to maintain an adequate distance. At the edge of the channel one may try, to the extent that the current permits it, to move toward the slope of the reef. With the correct swimming technique, exact buoyancy control, and proper equipment, it is possible to swim up this slope without tipping forward into the corals.
If it becomes absolutely necessary to grasp the coral, select a formation that is already dead.

PHOTOGRAPHY

When drifting along the reef, the photographer will be forced to do panoramic shots, inasmuch as the stops that can be made and any cross-current swimming can last only a few seconds. The very rare leaf fish, which never emerge from their grottoes, can be photographed with macro lenses, from 50- to 100-millemeter. Owners of *Motormarine II* and *Nikonos* camers should use the 1:3 macro equipment.

E - Majestic spotted eagle rays (Aetobatus narinari) *often ply the deeper waters around Miaru Faru.*

F, G - The thila *of Miaru Faru is also known as Shark Point, due to the presence of a great many grey reef sharks* (Carcharhinus amblyrhynchos).

H - A scattered group of Indian bannerfish (Heniochus pleurotaenia) *patrols the coral seabeds.*

G

H

EMBUDHU KANDU

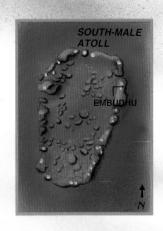

SOUTH-MALE
ATOLL

EMBUDHU

N

0 m

15 m

35 m

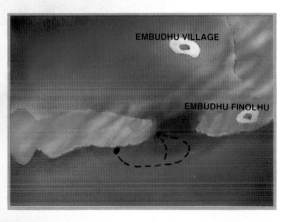

EMBUDHU VILLAGE

EMBUDHU FINOLHU

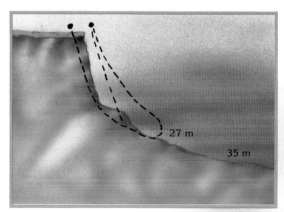

27 m

35 m

A

LOCATION

The diving site lies on the northeastern part of the South-Male Atoll. The specific site is the southern corner of the pass of Embudhu. The nearby islands, which both have a tourist village, are Embudhu and Embudhu Finolhu. The reef rises to within three meters (ten feet) of the surface, and then drops away, forming grottoes and crannies, especially around the channel. The ledge of the pass proper lies at a depth of thirty to thirty-five meters (one hundred to a hundred fifteen feet), and is quite bare, given the violent current that sometimes rushes through this funnel-shaped entrance to the atoll.

A - The broad pass of Embudhu is distinguished by the violent rush of the currents that provide a regular exchange of water on the interior of the lagoon.

B - A dense group of Maldive anemonefish (Amphiprion nigripes) swims around the tentacles of a large sea anemone.

C - Humphead wrasse (Cheilinus undulatus) are always quite sociable, and allow scuba divers to come quite close.

B

C

DIVES

Embudhu is a classic waiting dive, while the beginning and the conclusion are drift dives.
One enters the water over the outer wall of the atoll at a distance of about one hundred meters (three hundred thirty feet) from the corner of the channel. One then descends diagonally, keeping the wall to one's left, and then one reaches the outer edge of the slope. At this point, one should stop to observe, until the computer's safety curve or the air supply force one to surface.
One allows the current to drag one to the interior of the pass, taking great care to remain quite close to the left-hand wall, and one rises diagonally to the depth of five meters (sixteen feet) where, after making one's safety stop and inflating one's surface parachute, one can swim away from the reef, to be picked up by the diving-dhoni.

LIFE FORMS

Given the location and the enormous flow of water generated by the currents, Embudhu is a dive where one can see a "little bit of everything." The outer wall of the atoll is interrupted by a great many grottoes, where it is possible to observe the colorful inhabitants of the reef, from fish to soft coral. Once one has reached the ledge of the pass, one can see

D - The stonefish (Synanceia verrucosa) is one of the most dangerous inhabitants of the reef. Past master of camouflages, it bristles with spines that emit a powerful venom, which can be fatal in certain cases.

E - This scuba diver seems to chase a number of oriental sweetlips (Plectorhynchus orientalis) along the rock seabed.

F - With rapid strokes of their "wings," a great number of spotted eagle rays (Aetobatus narinari) swim away from the reef, toward the open ocean.

G - The hazy silhouette of a backlit scuba diver and a delicate alcionarian in a perfect illumination create a perfectly composed photograph.

the unmistakable silhouettes of grey reef sharks *(Carcharhinus amblyrhynchos)* in the dark-blue depths; after a first moment of timidity, these sharks begin to approach the scuba diver with curiosity; schools of eagle rays *(Aetobatus narinari)*, at times numbering as many as twenty-five individuals swimming in formation, hover in the water in line with the slope. It is possible to observe tuna *(Thunnus sp.)* of considerable size, jacks *(Caranx sp.)*, and, when the currents are weak, a family of humphead wrasse *(Cheilinus undulatus)* will accompany the divers from start to finish. After entering the channel, around the blocks of coral that have been detached from the wall, we will find schools of sweetlips *(Plectorhynchus sp.)*, of bluestriped snappers *(Lutjanus kasmira)*, snout pointing into the current. It is even possible to see, on the upper part of the reef, pairs of horned parrotfish *(Bolbometopon muricatum)*.

PHOTOGRAPHY

It is possible to take splendid photographs with wide-angle lenses of schools or eagle rays, both against the light, and in close-up,

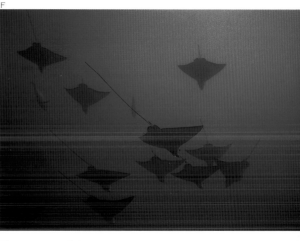

if one is careful to remain motionless and then to attract the curiosity of one or two individuals. The humphead wrasse also draw so close that it should be possible to take a handsome photograph of their snouts. With less extreme lenses, one should be able to take photographs of sharks and other deep-sea fish, especially during the middle of the day, when the light is best. On the interior of the channel, it is possible to take some beautiful photographs of bluestriped snappers, perhaps with a diver in the background.

THE FISH
OF THE MALDIVES

The coral seabeds of the Indian Ocean are found chiefly to the west, where the largest and richest coral formations are located. In particular, the archipelago of the Maldives constitute a particularly rich trove of coral; the island chain formed along the ridges of the peaks of the underwater mountains that have been given the same name; these submarine mountains are made up of a series of volcanoes that have formed the foundations of the numerous atolls that make up the Maldive Islands, also known as "the realm of the thousand islands". Located about eight hundred kilometers to the southwest of Sri Lanka, just north of the equator, and extending over an area measuring about eight hundred kilometers in length and about one hundred kilometers in breadth, the Republic of Maldives is made up of more than one thousand islands, for the most part uninhabited, and in some cases actually still undergoing the process of formation, as anyone who has an opportunity to sail around these islands is quickly made well aware. The islands are in reality constituted by a long chain of atolls, the coral formations that are characteristic of the Maldives and which actually take their name from this part of the Indian Ocean. The word "atoll," in fact, comes from the Maldivian word *atholu*, meaning "islands arranged in a ring." Atolls are considered by marine biologists to be one of the most complex of all coral formations, not only in terms of their structure but also in terms of the processes involved in their formation, which consists of the slow sinking of the original volcanic island or of the seabeds upon which the coral colonies develop. Whatever the formations may be that lead to the creation of an atoll, they host a series of environments that tend to recur with a certain regularity: a lagoon, a reef flat, a reef crest and a reef slope.

The lagoon consists of a flat, sandy, underwater area, which is bounded on one side by the beach of the adjacent island. Generally speaking, lagoons are none too deep and the coral formations found within them are limited in size and extent. The coral formations tend to expand along the outer boundaries, where they form a platform that abounds in species of coral that can withstand elevated levels of light and prolonged periods of exposure to the air, during low tides. As we move progressively out toward the open sea, the platform slopes downward, at first gently and then suddenly, until the first coral shelf, after which the seabed drops away toward the ocean depths. Each of these environments, naturally, has different ecological characteristics, but it takes time to learn to distinguish them. The shallow beds of the lagoon allow scubadivers to observe a number of species of gobies *(Nemateleotris sp.)*, which are quick to retreat into their dens, burrowed into the sand. Here and there, groups of large tropical goatfish *(Parupeneus sp.)* swim to and fro, easy to recognize because of the large barbles set beneath their mouths. It is by no means uncommon to encounter large eagle rays *(Aetobatus narinari)* or stingrays *(Taeniura melanospilos)*, especially in the early morning hours; these fish take refuge in the lagoons during the night.

The scattered coral formations made up of staghorn coral *(Acropora sp.)* or coral with a slightly more solid structure *(Porites sp.)* are ideal for observing in shallow waters the damselfish *(Dascyllus aruanus*, or *Domino damselfish)*, triggerfish *(Rhinecanthus aculeatus)*, and surgeonfish *(Zebrasoma veliferum)*, as well as a great number of *Labridae*. Where the coral belt becomes more extensive, the number of species of fish increases correspondingly: triggerfish, surgeonfish, parrotfish, Labridae, gobies, damselfish all populate the various ecological niches created in the coral labyrinths. Herbivorous and carnivorous species here find nourishment as well as areas in which they can find shelter and reproduce. The outer slope of the barrier reef is an extended decline toward the deep seabeds. Here one finds large anemones *(Heteractis sp.)* inhabited by clownfish *(Amphiprion sp.)* and the odd sea whip corals, perennially leaning in one direction or another, swept by the powerful currents typical of the passages that link the open ocean to the lagoons. Diving in this sort of area, in the company of expert guides, means being able to travel underwater at nearly the same speed as the fish themselves. Grey reef sharks *(Carcharhinus amblyrhynchos)*, whitetip reef sharks *(Carcharhinus albimarginatus)*, schools of jacks *(Caranx sp.)*, surgeonfish *(Zebrasoma sp.)*, tuna *(Thunnus sp.)*, barracuda *(Sphyraena sp.)*, eagle rays *(Aetobatus narinari)*, at times manta *(Manta birostris)*, and if you are particularly fortunate, even hammerhead sharks *(Sphyrna lewini)* and whale sharks *(Rhincodon typus)* can be found in these areas, where it is a matter of luck in most cases if you spot unusual species. Like shadows emerging from the blue depths, many of these species flit momentarily through the field of vision of scuba divers who, distracted by the virtually limitless variety of lifeforms (the species of fish alone found in these waters number more than a thousand), may miss the fleeting instant of opportunity. Not far from the reef, along the openings of underwater caverns, stand colonies of soft corals, the fans of the gorgonians upon which feather stars come to rest, or the ramified structures of *Dendrophyliidae*, blackish in hue and capable of staining wetsuits with their color. Beneath the coral formations or in the underwater grottos hide large groups of *Anthias* *(Pseudanthias squamipinnis)* or soldierfish *(Myripristis sp.)*, or groupers of a variety of species, observed from afar by large humphead wrasses *(Cheilinus undulatus)*, by batfish *(Platax teira)*, or by black *Odonus niger*, mid-sized triggerfish ready to flash away into the nearest niche or grotto, leaving only their filamentous tail emerging. If a diver lingers near an area sheltered from the current, then he is likely to see cleaner wrasse fish hard at work, and to note how the behavior and often the color of the fish being cleaned changes drastically, even in the space of a few minutes, or how the parrotfish *(Scaridae)* loudly crunch away at the coral, every so often releasing little clouds of coral sand which in time will turn into the pure white sand of an island in formation, ideally closing the circle between the land and the sea of the Maldives.

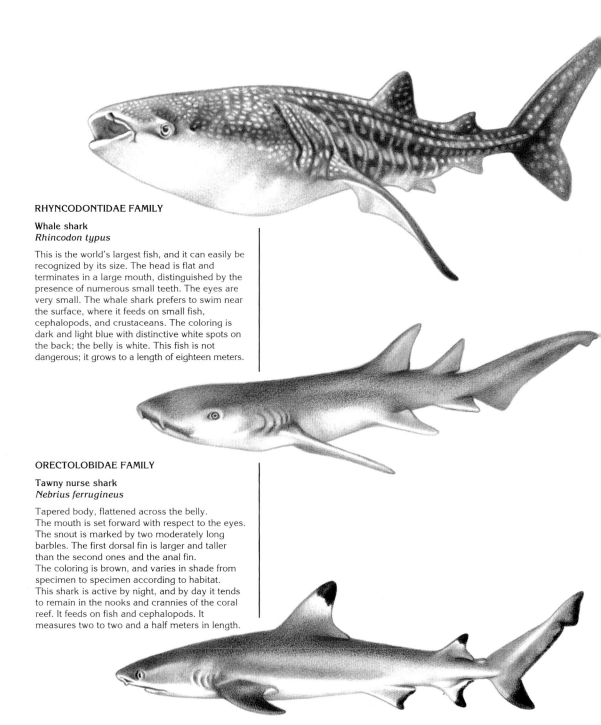

RHYNCODONTIDAE FAMILY

Whale shark
Rhincodon typus

This is the world's largest fish, and it can easily be recognized by its size. The head is flat and terminates in a large mouth, distinguished by the presence of numerous small teeth. The eyes are very small. The whale shark prefers to swim near the surface, where it feeds on small fish, cephalopods, and crustaceans. The coloring is dark and light blue with distinctive white spots on the back; the belly is white. This fish is not dangerous; it grows to a length of eighteen meters.

ORECTOLOBIDAE FAMILY

Tawny nurse shark
Nebrius ferrugineus

Tapered body, flattened across the belly.
The mouth is set forward with respect to the eyes.
The snout is marked by two moderately long barbles. The first dorsal fin is larger and taller than the second ones and the anal fin.
The coloring is brown, and varies in shade from specimen to specimen according to habitat.
This shark is active by night, and by day it tends to remain in the nooks and crannies of the coral reef. It feeds on fish and cephalopods. It measures two to two and a half meters in length.

CARCHARHINIDAE FAMILY   ✖

Blacktip reef shark
Carcharhinus melanopterus

Carcharhinid of moderate size, it is common in shallow coastal waters, especially near open sea reefs. The body is elongated; the snout is short and rounded; the head is flat. The tips of the fins are black. The teeth are triangular. The length is two meters. It seems to have territorial behavior.

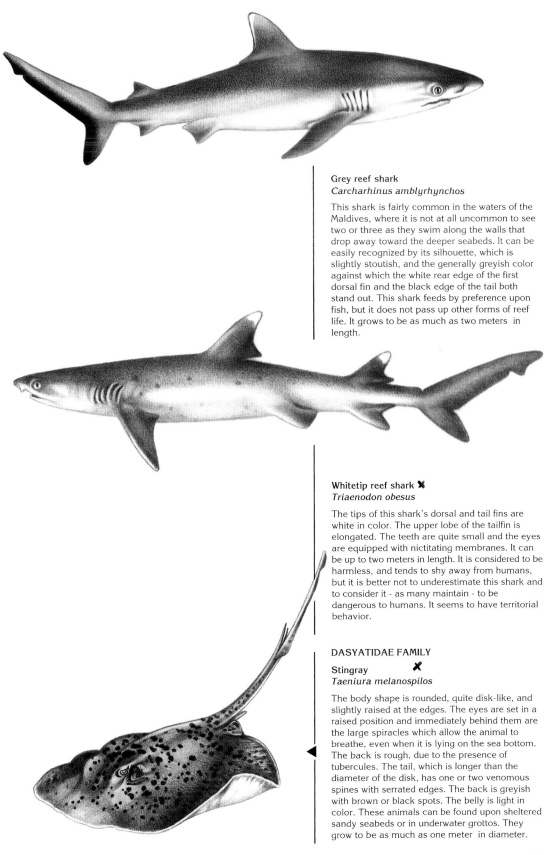

Grey reef shark
Carcharhinus amblyrhynchos

This shark is fairly common in the waters of the Maldives, where it is not at all uncommon to see two or three as they swim along the walls that drop away toward the deeper seabeds. It can be easily recognized by its silhouette, which is slightly stoutish, and the generally greyish color against which the white rear edge of the first dorsal fin and the black edge of the tail both stand out. This shark feeds by preference upon fish, but it does not pass up other forms of reef life. It grows to be as much as two meters in length.

Whitetip reef shark ✖
Triaenodon obesus

The tips of this shark's dorsal and tail fins are white in color. The upper lobe of the tailfin is elongated. The teeth are quite small and the eyes are equipped with nictitating membranes. It can be up to two meters in length. It is considered to be harmless, and tends to shy away from humans, but it is better not to underestimate this shark and to consider it - as many maintain - to be dangerous to humans. It seems to have territorial behavior.

DASYATIDAE FAMILY

Stingray ✖
Taeniura melanospilos

The body shape is rounded, quite disk-like, and slightly raised at the edges. The eyes are set in a raised position and immediately behind them are the large spiracles which allow the animal to breathe, even when it is lying on the sea bottom. The back is rough, due to the presence of tubercules. The tail, which is longer than the diameter of the disk, has one or two venomous spines with serrated edges. The back is greyish with brown or black spots. The belly is light in color. These animals can be found upon sheltered sandy seabeds or in underwater grottos. They grow to be as much as one meter in diameter.

MYLIOBATIDAE FAMILY

Spotted eagle ray
Aetobatus narinari

This ray can be recognized easily by the pointed and convex head with large eyes and broad lateral spiracles. The body is diamond-shaped and has broad, pointed pectoral fins. The tail, with one, two, or three denticulated spines, is about three times the length of the body. The ventral fins are broad and fleshy. The back is dark in coloring, with many small white spots. The disk-shaped body measures up to two meters in width. It attains a total length of up to two and a half meters. It can also be found in shallow lagoons (one to five meters in depth) on sandy bottoms.

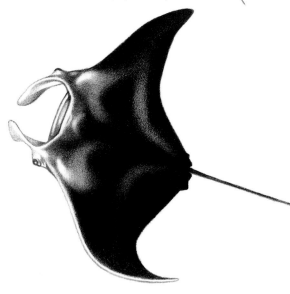

MOBULIDAE FAMILY

Giant manta X
Manta birostris

Easily recognized by the well developed pectoral fins, that can attain five to six meters in width. The head is projecting from the body, and is distinguished by a pair of long, flat, flexible cephalic fins, separated by the large arch of the mouth. The upper jaw is devoid of teeth. The spineless tail is long and slim. The dorsal coloring is dark, while the ventral coloring is quite light with dark blotches that can be referred to in order to distinguish one specimen from another.

SYNODONTIDAE FAMILY

Lizardfish
Synodus variegatus

Elongated body, compressed lengthwise. The head is convex toward the rear base. Eyes in an anterior-dorsal position. The snout is pointed, but short. The mouth is wide, and slightly oblique. The jaws are well developed and equipped with numerous needle-shaped teeth. The coloring is variable, but is generally brownish on the back with more or less distinct red spots on the sides. This fish prefers sandy bottoms where it waits in ambush, poised on its sizable ventral fins.

MURAENIDAE FAMILY

Honeycomb moray
Gymnothorax favagineus

This is a large variety of moray, but tapered in form. The head is conical and the snout is slightly pointed. When the mouth gapes open, it is possible to see the teeth, arranged in a single row, and more developed on the upper jaw. The fins are covered with a thick epidermis. The coloring is marked by many-sided dark splotches bordered in white or yellow so as to form a distinctive network pattern. This moray lives along the slopes of reefs, and can grow to be as long as one hundred eighty centimeters (seventy-one inches) in length.

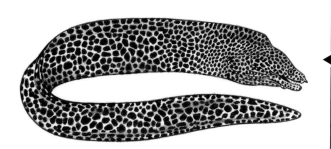

Leopard moray
Gymnothorax undulatus

Moray with a squat shape. The forward section of the animal appears rather large and tall, both because of the massive head and because of the dorsal fin that begins between the nape of what may be considered its neck and the gill aperture. The coloring of the body is marbled in appearance. The head is spotted. The edge of the gills and the tip of the tail are white. It lives amidst the nooks and crannies of the reef as well as in the flat areas and on the slopes. It measures up to 1.5 meters in length.

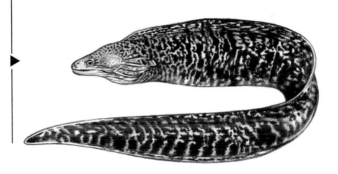

Giant moray
Gymnothorax javanicus

This is the largest of the morays and is fairly common all across the Maldives. The body is powerful, rather tall on the trunk, and ends in a very well developed head. The snout is short. The mouth is wide. The openings of the opercules are large and black and quite evident. The body is marked by three rows of dark brown spots. The tail is reticulated. It can grow to be as long as two and a half meters.

HETEROCONGRIDAE FAMILY

Black spotted gardeneel
Heteroconger hassi

These are extremely elusive creatures who flee immediately at the sight of an approaching scuba diver. They live in large colonies in sandy areas, generally deeper than twenty meters, and they allow the upper portion of their body to wave in the water, in search of the plankton on which they feed. The head is distinguished by a short snout, large eyes, and an oblique mouth with large lips. The body is light-colored and is spangled with numerous small dark spots, with larger spots close to the back. This species can grow to be forty centimeters in length.

HEMIRAMPHIDAE FAMILY

Halfbeak ✖
Hyporhamphus dussumieri

The fish of this species are easy to recognize because of their shape, which is reminiscent of that of the needle fish. The most distinctive feature, however, is that of the mouth, which has a long and slim lower jaw while the upper jaw is short and triangular in shape. These fish live in schools that move close to the surface of the water, where they hunt the smaller fish and plankton. The coloration is silvery, with bluish highlights on the back. They grow to be thirty centimeters in length.

FISTULARIDAE FAMILY

Cornetfish ✗
Fistularia commersonii

A cylindrical body that ends in a long and tubular snout.
The dorsal and anal fins are symmetrical and set quite far back. The two central rays of the caudal fin are very fine and elongated. The coloring is variable, due to the remarkable capacity for camouflage which this fish possesses and uses to capture - from ambush - the small prey on which it feeds. It is common to see this fish swim along, hidden by the body of a larger, but harmless, fish, so as to steal up unnoticed upon its prey. This fish measures up to a meter and a half in length.

AULOSTOMIDAE FAMILY

Trumpetfish ✗
Aulostoma chinensis

Elongated, compressed body which terminates in the front with a long and tubular snout, at the tip of which is a small mouth with a barble beneath the mandible. At the center of the back are a number of stout and erectile spines, the vestigial residue of the first dorsal fin. The second dorsal fin is located near the caudal peduncle, opposite from the anal fin. The coloration ranges from yellow to greenish. These fish feed on other smaller fish and crustaceans. They grow to be sixty centimeters in length.

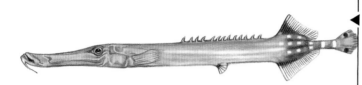

SYNGNATHIDAE FAMILY

Schultz's Pipefish ✗
Corythoichthys schultzi

This fish is rather difficult to see due to its mimetic color camouflage and its size.
The body is slender and the snout is very long. The eyes are large and well developed. The dorsal silhouette appears to be slightly serrated due to the configuration of the rigid rings that form the body of these fish. The caudal fin is reddish in color, with white edging. There are five rows of orange points along the length of the body. These fish live in the level areas of reefs and live on tiny crustaceans. They grow to be sixteen centimeters in length.

HOLOCENTRIDAE FAMILY

Blotcheye soldierfish ✗
Myripristis murdjan

Oval body, moderately compressed and high, covered with stinging scales. The first dorsal fin has some ten well developed spinous rays. The eyes are large. The mouth is wide.
The coloring is bright red. This is essentially a nocturnal fish, which remains at the entrance to its grotto during the day, as if it were keeping watch. It attains a length of up to thirty centimeters.

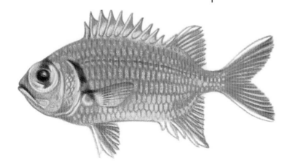

Crown squirrelfish ✗
Sargocentron diadema

Oval body, longer and less tall than that of the *Sargocentron diadema* and the *S. spiniferum* species. The eyes are quite large, as this too is a species with nocturnal habits. The coloring is red, with evident white stripes on the sides. A white band runs around the lower portion of the face as far as to the opercules. The forward section of the dorsal fin is black. It measures twenty-five centimeters in length.

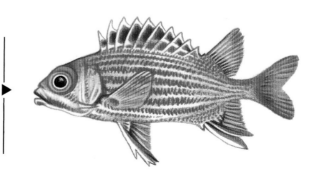

Sabre squirrelfish
Sargocentron spiniferum ✗

Its body is moderately compressed and tall; the snout is pointed with relatively large eyes. The dorsal fin is well developed with red interradial membranes. Coloring of the body is red with spots of the same color, but darker on the opercula and at the base of the pectoral fins. This is a nocturnal species, and it is aggressive by nature, due to its territorial habits. It measures up to forty-five centimeters in length.

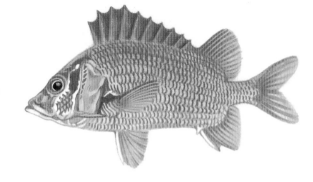

SCORPAENIDAE FAMILY ✗

Clearfin turkeyfish
Pterois radiata

Oblong body with a large head and a large mouth. The rays of the pectoral fins are very long, do not branch out, and the upper ones are joined by a membrane but only at the base. All of the rays are poisonous. The body is a brownish red with white stripes. Above the eyes there are long fleshy papillae. It can attain a size of 25 centimeters.

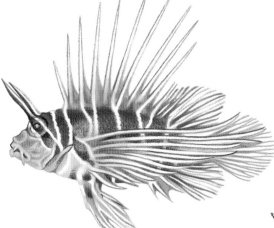

Turkeyfish
Pterois volitans ✗

Body is similar to the previous species. The coloring presents broad brown vertical stripes; not all the same width. The rays of the fins are not naked, but possess a more or less developed membrane that makes them similar to feathers. The odd-numbered fins bear rows of brownish-black spots. Around the mouth and above the eyes one can clearly see some indented appendages.

Devil scorpionfish
Scorpaenopsis diabolus

A slightly oval body, massive and high, with fleshy excrescences. The head is large and is covered with spines; the mouth is wide and turns upwards. The pectoral fins extend to the anal fin. The coloring provides excellent camouflage, as this is a species that hunts from ambush. The tailfin has broad dark vertical stripes. The spines of the dorsal fin are poisonous. It grows to a length of thirty centimeters.

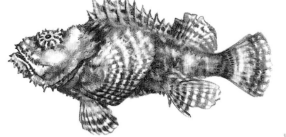

Leaf scorpionfish
Taenianotus triacanthus

The shape of the body is similar to that of a scorpionfish, with a large head, oblique mouth, and compression and tapering toward the rear. The upper section of the eye is distinguished by fragmented appendices. The dorsal fin is very large, and the spinous rays are venomous. The coloration is quite variable and mimetic and allows the fish to advance slowly, like a leaf borne on the current, upon the smaller fish upon which it feeds. It grows to be ten to twelve centimeters in length.

141

SERRANIDAE FAMILY

Yellowtail fairy-basslet
Pseudanthias evansi X

Oval and compressed body. Conical head that terminates in a mouth. Long dorsal fin and lunate caudal fin with well-developed, pointed lobes. Large pectoral and ventral fins. The coloration is particularly distinctive: the upper part of the body and the tail are yellow, while the rest of the body is violet. A purple striation runs from the tip of the snout to the base of the pectoral fins, cutting across the eyes. These fish live in schools near the upper section of the outer barrier reef. They grow to be seven centimeters in length.

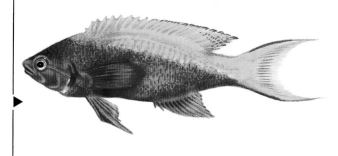

Redmouth grouper
Aethaloperca rogaa X

Grouper with stout, tall, compressed shape. The head is large and the dorsal profile appears to be concave, in line with the eyes. The mouth is large and the lips are thick. Adults of this species have a sort of hump. The dorsal, anal, and caudal fins have a straight rear edge. The coloration is uniformly dark brown. The mouth and the opercules appear to be reddish. In the young of this species, the tail has a white edging. These fish live on other fish, and live along the reef. They grow to be sixty centimeters in length.

Smalltooth grouper
Epinephelus microdon

Spindle-shaped body typical of groupers. Massive head, short snout, and relatively small eyes. Slightly jutting mandible and large mouth. Upper edge of the opercules is slightly curved. The lower edge of the caudal fin is rounded. The coloration is mottled in white and dark brown with five large dark spots in the dorsal area. It lives on crustaceans and fish. This fish grows to be sixty centimeters (about twenty-four inches) in length.

Black-saddled coraltrout
Plectropomus laevis

Relatively elongated body, spindle-shaped and compressed. Massive head with a straight dorsal silhouette. Large, oblique mouth that allows one to see the large canine-like teeth of the upper jaw. The broad caudal fin has a virtually straight edge. The coloration is reddish-brown with small light-colored splotches on the body and on the caudal fin. A number of large dark splotches stand out on the back, but no further down than the middle of the flanks. This fish lives in the deeper areas of the reef, and grows to be ninety centimeters in length.

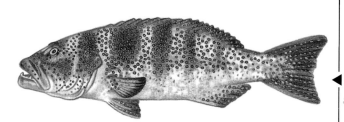

Four-saddle grouper
Epinephelus spilotoceps

Grouper with a tall body that tapers toward the rear. The head is massive, with large eyes and a short snout with a blunt profile. The basic coloration is light, but there are dark or reddish spots that stand out against the background; these spots are roughly hexagonal or polygonal, and are edged with white. At the base of the dorsal fin, one may note four large dark splotches. Among the groupers of the Maldives, this is one of the smallest, and grows to be no longer than thirty centimeters.

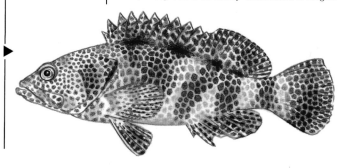

Scalefin anthias
Pseudanthias squamipinnis

Oval, compressed body, which ends in a sickle-shaped tail with elongated lobes. The snout is short and rounded, and the mouth is terminal. The dorsal fin is well developed, especially in the male, which has several particularly long fore rays. The coloring is reddish, with red spots near the pectoral fins. The females have yellowish shadings. This fish is gregarious, and forms schools dominated by one or two males. They attain a length of fifteen to seventeen centimeters.

Peacock grouper
Cephalopholis argus

The body is massive, tapered, and slightly compressed. The head is powerful, with a slightly prominent lower jaw. The edge of the caudal fin is rounded. The dorsal fin has nine spinous rays and a rounded rear edge that ends in proximity of the caudal peduncle and opposite the anal fin. The coloring is marked by numerous dark blue spots and by ten dark bands on the sides. The fins are dark blue. These fish attain a length of fifty centimeters.

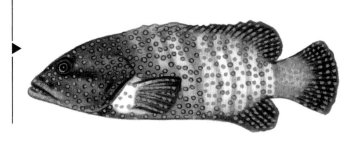

Coral grouper
Cephalopholis miniata

The body is similar to that of *C. argus*. The rear edges of the dorsal and anal fins are less rounded than in the previous species. The coloring is a very bright reddish-orange, with numerous small dark-blue ocellate spots scattered all over the body and fins, and tends to become darker in the adults. A fairly territorial species, it prefers to remain in the general vicinity of grottoes and underwater crannies. According to some observations, this fish tends to become gregarious during the mating season, and to gather to restrict areas. It attains a length of forty to forty-five centimeters.

Lunartail grouper
Variola louti

Tapered body which terminates toward the rear with a tall caudal peduncle supporting an unmistakable tail in the form of a crescent moon or sickle, and with elongated lobes. Dorsal and anal fins have pointed rear edges. The coloring is reddish or brownish, with purple highlights and numerous pale spots. This is a fairly common species and attains lengths of up to eighty or eighty-five centimeters.

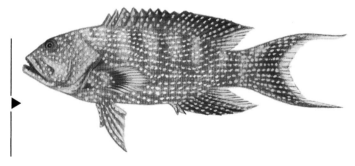

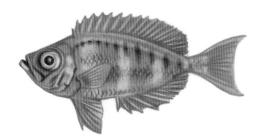

Goggle eye
Priacanthus hamrur

The body is oval, tall, and compressed. The snout is short, and the large eyes stand out, revealing the nocturnal habits of the species. The mouth is turned upward. The caudal fin is shaped like a crescent moon, with elongated lobes, especially in the adults of the species. The coloring is generally a dark reddish hue, but can change rapidly, acquiring more or less pronounced silvery highlights or becoming striped with red on silvery body. The dorsal and anal fins have dark highlights along their edges. This fish attains a length of forty to forty-five centimeters.

CIRRHITIDAE FAMILY

Pixy hawkfish
Cirrhitichthys oxycephalus

The body is massive, tall, and more compressed toward the front. The dorsal profile appears to be concave in line with the eyes, which tend to protrude slightly, so as to allow the fish to observe its surroundings when it remains resting on the bottom. The dorsal fin has fringing at the tip of the spinous rays. The coloring is whitish, with dark brown spots edged with red. The fins are spangled with red. It feeds chiefly on small crustaceans, and grows to a length of seven centimeters.

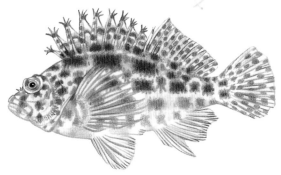

Longnose hawkfish
Oxycirrhites typus

The body is slightly cylindrical, taller at the center, and terminates in an elongated snout. The mouth is small. The spinous part of the dorsal fin bears a series of appendages. Pectoral fins are particularly well developed, and this fish uses them to balance upon gorgonians. Here the fish is perfectly camouflaged, due to a series of red stripes that form a checkerboard on its body. It attains a length of between ten and thirteen centimeters.

CARANGIDAE FAMILY

Bluefin Trevally ✘
Caranx melampygus

The body is elongated, and rather tall; forward, it terminates with a convex head and a high forehead. The eyes are small. The caudal peduncle is narrow and reinforced with visible bony plates, the lateral line is complete and arched anteriorly. The coloring is greenish-brown, with numerous small black spots. The long, sickle-shaped pectoral fins with scales on their sides are yellow in the young of the species. This fish grows to be longer than one meter.

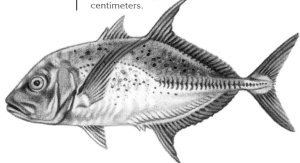

Bigeye Trevally ✘
Caranx sexfasciatus

The body is elongated and compressed; the forward silhouette is rounded. The lower jaw tends to jut. On the caudal stalk, there are evident keels; the caudal fin is sharply forked. The coloring is blue-gray or blue-green on the back. The lobes of the caudal fin show a blackish hue. The sides are greenish-yellow or silvery. The young of the species are golden yellow, with four to seven broad dark vertical bands. This fish grows to be longer than a meter and a half.

LUTJANIDAE FAMILY

Bluestriped snapper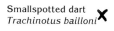
Lutjanus kasmira

Tapered body with pointed snout. Large eyes and mouth. The dorsal fin extends to the height of the caudal peduncle. The coloring is golden yellow on the back, becoming gradually paler along the sides and almost silvery on the belly. Typical of the species are the four light stripes running lengthwise; the longest of the stripes runs from the mouth to the caudal peduncle. The edges of the dorsal and the caudal fins are black. This fish measures forty centimeters in length.

Smallspotted dart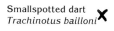
Trachinotus bailloni

The body is oval and compressed. The head has a blunt profile and a short snout. The mouth is terminal. The first dorsal fin is reduced to no more than spinous rays not joined by membrane. The second dorsal fin and the anal fin are opposed and are very long. The caudal fin is deeply incised, with pointed lobes. The coloration is silvery, with grey-green shading on the back. Along the lateral line there are two to five rounded black spots. The forward edges of the odd-numbered fins are blue-black in color. This fish can often be found inside lagoons. They grow to be thirty centimeters in length.

Humpback red snapper
Lutjanus gibbus

The body is massive, tall, and compressed. The snout is pointed, but in the larger individuals, the dorsal profile presents a distinctive concavity in line with the eyes. The pre-operculum presents a deep incisure. The caudal fin is sharply incised and has rounded lobes. The coloration is brownish-green on the back, and becomes reddish on the sides and on the belly. The pattern of the scales gives the sides a reticulated appearance. The eyes, the lips, and the base of the pectoral fins are yellow in color. These fish live in schools at a considerable depth along the reef. They reach a length of forty centimeters.

Two-spot red snapper
Lutjanus bohar

The body is massive, fairly tall, and rounded. The eyes are large and the mouth is wide, with sharp canine-like teeth. The pre-operculum presents a slight incisure. The caudal fin is broad and slightly incised. The pectoral fins are sickle-shaped and well developed. The dorsal coloration is reddish-bronze, while the ventral coloring is lighter. At the base of the dorsal fin, there are two distinct mother-of-pearl-colored splotches. This fish lives in the deeper areas of the barrier reef. It grows to be fifty centimeters in length.

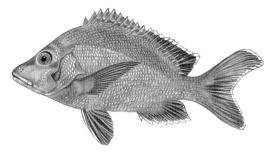

CAESIONIDAE FAMILY

Yellowfin fusilier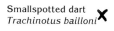
Caesio xanthonota

The body is oval, elongated, and compressed. The snout is short and the mouth is small, lined with small teeth. The dorsal fin is long. The caudal fin is profoundly incised, with pointed lobes. The upper portion of the body and the caudal fin are yellow in color. The lower half is light-blue in color. The eyes are red. The base of the pectoral fins is black, the edges of the caudal, analy are pinkish. This fish lives in schools along the exposed side of the reef. They grow to be thirty centimeters in length.

LETHRINIDAE FAMILY

Blackspot emperor
Lethrinus harak ◄

The shape of the body, which is fairly tall and compressed, is reminiscent of that of Mediterranean sea bream. The dorsal profile of the head is slightly tilted; the snout is pointed. The caudal fin is slightly incised, and has pointed lobes. The coloration is grey, with greenish-yellow highlights. At the center of the flanks, one may note an oblong black spot, edged in yellow. The dorsal, anal, and caudal fins have red highlights. This fish feeds upon benthic invertebrates and lives inside lagoons and on level seabeds. It grows to be sixty centimeters in length.

MULLIDAE FAMILY

Yellowsaddle goatfish
Parupeneus cyclostomus

The high, tapered body ends in a jutting snout. The lower jaw is distinguished by the presence of two long barbles that extend back to the ventral fins. The two dorsal fins are sharply separated. The tail is typically two-lobed. The head has bluish stripes that are fairly evident. The second dorsal fin has a dark spot toward the rear. The coloring is brighter in the young. It measures thirty-five centimeters in length.

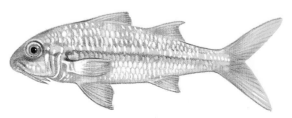

HAEMULIDAE FAMILY

Oriental sweetlips ✗
Plectorhynchus orientalis

The body is oblong, tall, and compressed. The head is rounded and the snout is short. The mouth is small and the lips are thick. The flanks are distinguished by six or seven black striations lengthwise; the two central striations extend all the way to the caudal fin. The snout is yellow, as are the fins, which are spotted with black. These fish tend to form small groups, which stay motionless, in the shelter of the larger coral formations. They feed upon mollusks and crustaceans. These fish grow to be fifty centimeters in length.

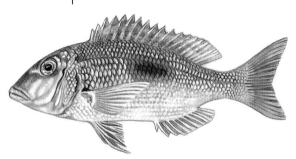

EPHIPPIDAE FAMILY

Batfish ✗
Platax teira

The body is very tall and compressed, so that the adult of the species actually resembles a disk. The forward profile of the head is convex and smooth, but it is broken in line with the snout, which becomes progressively longer. The young of the species have very tall and narrow dorsal and anal fins, but over time these become rounded and shorter. The coloration also varies with age. The young are reddish or yellowish-brown, while the adults display broad dark vertical bands, or else are more or less silvery, while parts of their fins are dark in color. They live in small schools and are omnivorous. They grow to be fifty centimeters in length.

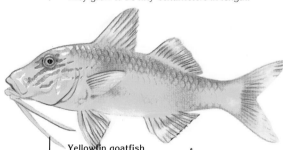

Yellowfin goatfish ↙
Mulloides vanicolensis

The body is elongated, nearly flat, and higher toward the front. The profile of the head is oblique. The mouth is small and beneath the jaw are the distinctive barbles that are characteristic of the family. There are two dorsal, clearly formed dorsal fins The caudal fin is forked. The coloration is characterized by lateral striations that vary in color: yellow, orange, or red in some cases. The sides of the snout are suffused with red or orange. The fins are pinkish. This species lives in schools near sandy seabeds. They grow to be thirty-five to forty centimeters in length.

SPHYRAENIDAE FAMILY

Great barracuda
Sphyraena barracuda

The body is elongated and slightly cylindrical. The snout is long and pointed, and the lower jaw is prominent. The teeth are numerous and canine-shaped. There are two dorsal fins, clearly separated. The coloring ranges from greyish to greenish-brown on the back, while the sides and the belly are silvery. The adults have irregular dark spots along their sides near the caudal fin. This species attains a length of 1.5 to 1.8 meters.

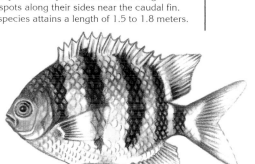

POMACENTRIDAE FAMILY

Sergeant major
Abudefduf saxatilis

Compressed body, ovoid in shape and fairly tall, covered with rough scales which extend to the fins. The greyish silvery coloring shifts toward bright yellow on the back. Along the sides of the fish, there are five dark vertical bands, the first of which intersects the rearmost edge of the operculum. The coloring becomes lighter when the fish lives near sandy seabeds, and darker near coral. Adult males acquire bluish and purplish nuances when they are guarding the spawn. They attain a length of ten to fifteen centimeters.

Bluegreen chromis
Chromis viridis

The shape of the body is roughly similar to the damselfish of the Mediterranean. The coloring tends to bluish, and is relatively intense, with slight nuances along the edge of the scales. This fish is gregarious, and tends to form large groups, each of which seems to colonize a specific coral formation, favoring those near the sheer walls at the outer edge of the reef. They measure from eight to ten centimeters in length.

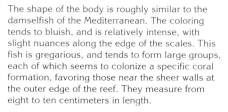

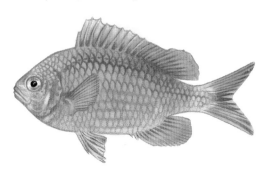

Half-and-half chromis
Chromis dimidiata

The shape of the body is similar to the species described immediately above. The coloring, however, is radically different, and allows one to recognize this species quite easily; half the body is white and half is dark brown or black. This fish is gregarious, and tends to form huge schools near large coral formations, venturing to greater depths than the *C. viridis*. It measures seven centimeters in length.

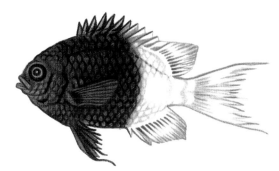

Banded dascyllus
Dascyllus aruanus

The body is fairly stubby, squarish, tall, and compressed. The mouth is small with a slightly prominent lower jaw. The background coloring is whitish, with three distinctive diagonal dark bands, the first of which covers the eye and the mouth. This fish forms small groups, each of which is closely associated with a single coral colony. Only larger specimens venture at any distance from the corals, while smaller ones remain in permanent residence among the branches. They measure eight to ten centimeters in length.

Black-footed clownfish
Amphiprion nigripes

The body is oval, stout, and tall, and is covered with large scales. The dorsal profile of the head presents a saddle formation above the eyes. The snout is brief; the mouth is small and terminal. The dorsal fin is long, but short. The caudal fin has a rounded upper edge. The coloration ranges from orange to yellow, but there is always a white strip on the head. The ventral fins are black. This fish lives in symbiosis with the genus *Heteractis*. They grow to be seven or eight centimeters in length.

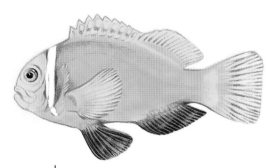

Domino damselfish
Dascyllus trimaculatus

The shape of the body is typical of the genus. The mouth is small, considering that this is a fish feeding on plankton. The coloring is the most distinctive feature, and quite sufficient to make the fish unmistakable. In fact, this species is either completely black or dark brown, with three white spots: one on either side and a third on the forehead. These spots are most pronounced in the young, and tend to fade in adulthood. The species is quite common around anemonefish, amidst long-spined black urchins *(Diadema antillarum)*, and amidst acroporas. It measures up to fourteen centimeters in length.

Clark's anemonefish
Amphiprion clarkii

The shape of the body is similar to that of other clownfish. The coloration is variable, but is generally quite dark. Two white strips are always present along the flanks, and often there is another one on the caudal peduncle. The caudal fin can be white or yellow. The ventral and anal fins are black. The young of this species have a white snout. These fish live in association with large, short-tentacled anemones. They are omnivorous and reproduce in the period between fall and summer. They grow to a length of fifteen centimeters.

Indian damselfish
Pomacentrus indicus

Ovoid, compressed, tall body. Short and arched snout. The mouth has conical teeth arranged in two rows. The dorsal fin is long, and its rear edge partly overtowers the caudal peduncle; the anal fin is also particularly well developed, and is pointed toward the rear. The caudal fin is slightly incised. The coloration is dark, with light splotches at the center of the scales on the flanks and a black spot at the base of the pectoral fins. The young are bluish, with a yellow spot on what corresponds to the nape of the neck. They grow to be nine centimeters in length.

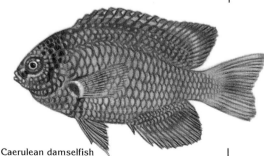

Caerulean damselfish
Pomacentrus caeruleus

The shape of the body is typical of the Pomacentrus genus. The snout is short and the mouth is small and terminal. The dorsal and anal fins have pointed rear edges which extend over the caudal peduncle. The caudal fin is bilobed and slightly incised. The coloration is light blue on the flanks and on the back. The belly and the caudal peduncle are yellow. The rear of the tail is edged in blue. This species is omnivorous, and lives among the corals on level seabeds and on the edges of reefs. They grow to be seven centimeters in length.

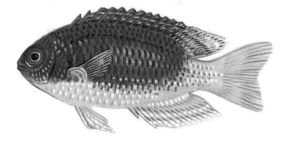

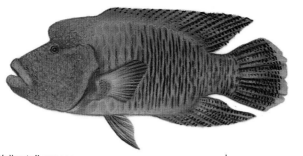

Humphead wrasse
Cheilinus undulatus

The humphead wrasse is the largest known member of the *Labridae* family, and has a very distinctive tall and stubby structure. The mouth is large and features thick protractile lips which allow this fish literally to suck up its prey. In the adults, the head is marked by a pronounced bump on the forehead. The greenish-grey coloring has irregular greenish-yellow stripes along the sides, shifting to orange on the head. These fish can be as long as two meters, and can weigh more than 170-180 kilograms.

Yellowtail wrasse
Anampses meleagrides

Tapered body, with a generally oval silhouette, and with a slight frontal hump, more pronounced in females. The mouth is terminal, and protractile, with large fleshy lips. The coloring of adult males is dark and purplish with more-or-less elongated bluish spots along the edge of the scales. Dorsal and anal fins feature bluish stripes, as does the rearmost edge of the caudal fin, the lobes of which are elongated. Females have a dark coloring, spangled with numerous white spots. The snout and the lower head are reddish. The caudal fin is yellow. This fish measures up to twenty-five centimeters in length.

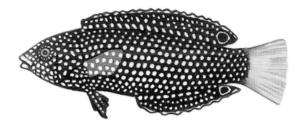

Moon wrasse
Thalassoma lunare

The body is tapered, powerful, and slightly compressed. The head is rounded, the snout is short. The mouth is small and the lips are thin. The caudal fin is truncated in the young; partially moon-shaped in adults, especially larger males, which are also bluish. The coloring is greenish with vertical purplish-red stripes on the sides. The head is greenish-blue with broad pink bands running roughly lengthwise. The caudal fin is yellowish at the center with pink stripes along the lobes. It attains a length of twenty-five to thirty centimeters.

Redbreasted Maori wrasse
Cheilinus fasciatus

The body is compressed and stout, and is taller toward the front. The head is massive with a blunt profile. The mouth is slightly oblique, with large lips and well developed anterior teeth. The rear edge of the dorsal fin has elongated rays. The caudal fin has elongated lobes. The head and the body are orange-red as far back as the ventral fins. The flanks are distinguished by six or seven dark bands, edged with white, which extend as far as the dorsal fin; one can see small red dots on them. This fish feeds upon benthic invertebrates and can grow to be thirty centimeters in length.

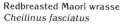

Cleaner wrasse
Labroides dimidiatus

The body is compressed, elongated, and covered with large scales. The head is pointy; the snout is elongated, with a small terminal mouth lined with numerous small and pointed teeth. The upper jaw is longer than the lower. The forward half of the body is brownish, and darker on the back than on the belly. A broad black band runs from the beginning of the snout all the way to the tip of the caudal fin, widening as it goes. The base of the anal fin and the rear part of the body are an intense dark blue. It attains a length of ten centimeters.

Checkerboard wrasse
Halichoeres hortulanus ✗

The body is elongated, ovoid, and compressed. The head is well developed and the snout is pointed. The mouth is terminal. The individuals of this species changes gender, from female to male, as they grow. The males have a green head with orange-pink bands and spots which extend as far as the base of the pectoral fins. The body is blue-green, with dark spots at the center of the scales. The tail is edged with red. The female has a yellow tail, the rear part of the body is reddish and presents a black splotch on the back. These fish grow to be twenty-five centimeters in length.

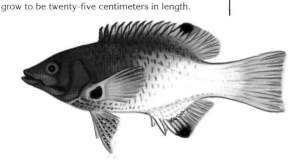

Axilspot hogfish
Bodianus axillaris

It has a tapered and compressed body with a pointed snout. The ventral fins are well developed and the longer ventral rays reach almost to the anal aperture. The caudal fin is truncated in adults and rounded in the young. The forward portion of the body is dark and contrasts sharply with the lighter hue of the rest. The base of the pectoral, dorsal and anal fins have a pronounced dark spot. The young specimens have nine white spots on their bodies. They reach twenty centimeters in length.

Bird wrasse
Gomphosus caeruleus

A typically oval body, slightly compressed. The snout is distinctively elongated and tubular in the adults. The mouth is terminal, but sufficiently well developed to prey on small animals. The caudal fin is rounded, but tends to develop elongated lobes with time. The coloring is dark blue in males. Females are green on their backs and yellowish on their bellies, with black spots on their sides. They measure from twenty to twenty-five centimeters in length.

SCARIDAE FAMILY

Steephead parrotfish
Scarus gibbus

The body is oval, tall, and powerful. The head has a forward silhouette that is quite convex, and nearly vertical. The dental plates are not particularly pronounced. On the cheeks, are three rows of large scales. The caudal fin is semilunar. The coloring is brownish yellow, while the lower part of the snout is green in the females. On the scales, are fairly intense pink stripes. These remain in males as well; males have on their dorsal area a greenish coloring with touches of violet. The ventral section is blue-green. The rear of the caudal fin has a green edge. It attains a length of seventy centimeters.

Flame parrotfish ✗
Scarus ghobban

The body is oval, tall, and slightly compressed. The snout is rounded. The lips are thick and in some points allow one to see the white teeth. The caudal peduncle is short and powerful. The caudal fin is slightly lunate, with pointed lobes. The females generally have a coloration with a foundation of reddish-yellow and vertical dark blue bands. The male has no dark blue bands, but it does have striations of this color on the lips and from the mouth to the eye. The scales on the body are edged in dark blue. The odd-numbered fins are suffused in red. They grow to be sixty centimeters in length.

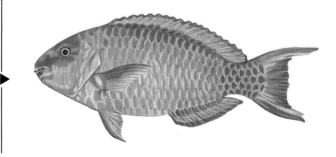

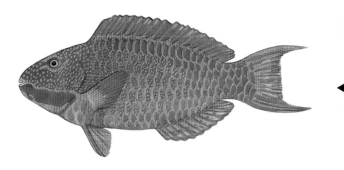

Bicolor parrotfish
Cetoscarus bicolor

The body is generally spindle-shaped and oval. The snout is pointed. The caudal fin is lunate with pointed lobes. The female of the species is dark in coloration, dark brown on the back and lighter in color on the flanks, where the scales have a light spot at the center, and speckled. The males have a dark-bluish head, which has a very fine speckling of fuchsia. The back and part of the flanks are green, while the edge of the scales is fuchsia. The fish of this species grow to be as much as one meter in length.

Bullethead parrotfish
Scarus sordidus

The general configuration of the body is typical of parrotfish. The dental plates can be clearly seen. The young present a pattern of coloring with horizontal stripes. As they grow, this coloring turns dark brown. The adult males are green in color, and the edges of their scales are salmon pink. The cheeks are bright orange, fading to yellow on the opercula. Strangely, their teeth are green, while the female of the species has a pink mouth.

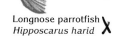

Longnose parrotfish
Hipposcarus harid

The body is oval and slender. The dorsal profile of the head is rather rectilinear. The snout is long and pointed. The caudal fin is typically lunate with long lobes, particularly in the larger males. The female has a bronzed coloration which is lighter in color on the belly, and yellowish dorsal and anal fins, edged with a bluish shade, with a caudal fin edged in dark blue. The male is light green, with scales edged in orange. The lips and the edges of the odd-numbered fins have a double band colored orange and dark blue. This species can grow to be forty centimeters in length.

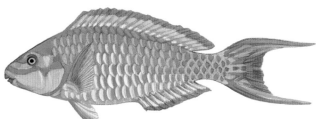

CHAETODONTIDAE FAMILY

Indian butterflyfish
Chaetodon mitratus

The body is tall and compressed, The dorsal profile of the head is rectilinear, and is slightly convex in line with the eyes. The snout is pointed. The back is sharply angled. The dorsal fin has the first spinous rays very well developed and distinct one from another. The pectoral fins are large and the anal has distinct spinous rays. The eyes are masked by a dark band. The coloration of the flanks is white with two broad dark oblique bands, the second of which extends to the dorsal fin as well; the rays of this fin have a white tip. Grows to be as long as twelve centimeters.

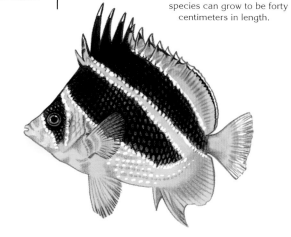

Threadfin butterflyfish
Chaetodon auriga

The body is nearly rectangular, very tall and compressed. The head is concave toward the front, and terminates in a pointed, short snout. A broad dark band covers the eye, narrowing on the back. The dorsal fin features a dark ocellate spot along the rearmost edge, topped by a number of elongated and filamentous rays which constitute one of the distinctive features of this species. The *C. auriga* swims alone or in pairs. It measures twenty to twenty-five centimeters in length.

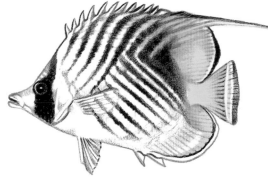

Racoon butterflyfish
Chaetodon lunula

The body is tall, compressed, oval, and slightly rounded toward the back. The dorsal profile of the head is concave. The snout is short and pointed. A broad black band edged with white masks the eyes. On the caudal peduncle, there is a black spot. The upper part of the flanks is more or less dark, and oblique striations run from here toward the belly. This species is nocturnal and omnivorous, and lives on the edges of the reef. These fish grow to be twenty centimeters in length.

Madagascar butterflyfish
Chaetodon madagascariensis

The body tends to be oval in shape. The dorsal profile of the head is rectilinear or slightly convex over what would be the nape of the neck, and concave above the nostrils. The snout is short and pointed. The teeth are arranged in well spaced rows. The basic coloration is light. A black band extends over the eyes, and on what would be the the nape of the neck there is a dark horseshoe-shaped spot. The flanks are adorned with six to eight angled black striations. The posterior portion of the body is marked by an orange band, which reappears on the tail, and which extends from the dorsal to the anal fin. This species is omnivorous, and lives along the slope of the reef. These fish grow to be fourteen centimeters in length.

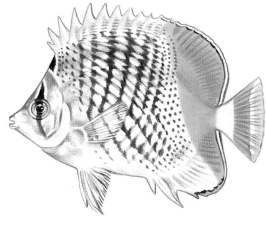

Black-backed butterflyfish
Chaetodon melannotus

The body is tall, compressed, and rounded in shape. The dorsal profile of the head is rectilinear, and slightly concave at the beginning of the snout. The eyes are in part hidden by a narrow black band. The upper part of the caudal peduncle and the forward portion of the anal fin each have a black spot. The body is light colored and is adorned with narrow black striations made up of dense black speckles. The fins are yellow. This fish lives on Alcyonarians, and grows to be fourteen centimeters in length.

Double-saddled butterflyfish
Chaetodon falcula

The body is compressed and oval. The dorsal profile of the head is concave. The snout is long and pointed. The eyes are masked by a black band. On the back one notes two large saddle-shape splotches. The odd-numbered fins are yellow. The caudal peduncle is adorned by a dark ring. The body is whitish, with dark vertical striations. This fish almost always lives in pairs, and feeds upon invertebrates. It prefers the shallower areas of the reef. It grows to be eighteen centimeters in length.

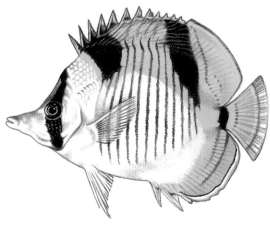

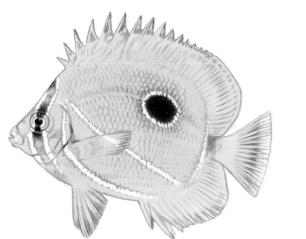

Bennett's Butterflyfish
Chaetodon bennetti

The body is rounded, tall, and compressed. The dorsal profile of the head is quite inclined and slightly concave. The snout is short. The mouth is small and terminal. The basic coloration is yellow, and upon this base there stands out a large black ocellate splotch, edged with light blue. Two oblique light-blue striations extend from the base of the pectoral fin toward the anal fin. The eyes are hidden by a black band edged with light blue. This species lives in pairs and is more common on the outer part of the reef. They grow to be fourteen centimeters in length.

Long-nosed butterflyfish
Forcipiger longirostris

This fish is extremely distinctive in shape, easy to recognize by the long beak-like snout and the truncated rear portion of the body. The upper section of the head is black, while the lower section is lighter in color, with silvery highlights. The body is yellow, with a few dark stripes at the base of the pectoral fin. The caudal fin is transparent. These fish live in small groups made up of five to six individuals, and feeds on small invertebrates that it captures in the nooks and crannies of the coral with its long snout. They grow to be eighteen centimeters in length.

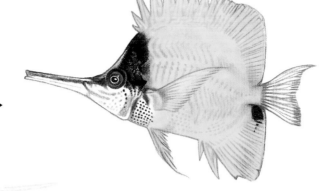

Bannerfish ✖
Heniochus diphreutes

A tall, disk-shaped body, greatly compressed and truncated in the rear. The head has a concave profile. The snout is short and the eyes are large. The coloring is whitish, with two broad dark bands on the sides, which limit the higher and more developed part of the dorsal fin, well extended behind. A dark band partially covers the eyes. The rear sections of the dorsal and caudal fins are yellow. Unlike most butterflyfish, they feed on plankton. They grow to be sixteen centimeters in length.

Triangular butterflyfish
Chaetodon triangulum

The body is tall and compressed. The dorsal profile of the head is straight-edged and quite inclined. The snout is short. The coloration of the body, which is whitish toward the front, becomes progressively darker as one moves back. The snout is reddish-brown. A strip of the same color masks the eyes and is followed by another, thinner strip. The flanks are adorned with dark striations. The caudal peduncle has a yellow strip. The dorsal and anal fins are edged with light blue. The caudal fin is yellow and black. These fish live in pairs and feed on the polyps of coral, with which it tends to live. These fish grow to a length of fifteen centimeters.

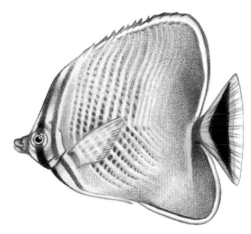

153

Masked bannerfish
Heniochus monoceros ✗

The body is tall, slightly oval, and compressed. The head is massive, with a distinctively concave dorsal profile, between the base of the dorsal fin and the eye. The snout is short and pointed. The rear edge of the dorsal and the anal fin is rounded. The fourth ray of the dorsal fin is very long and well developed, especially in the adult males of the species. The caudal fin is truncated. The coloration is characterized by three dark bands separated by white areas. The dorsal and caudal fins are yellow. These fish live in pairs or in small groups along the outer part of the reef. They grow to be twenty-five centimeters in length.

Black Pyramid butterflyfish ✗
Hemitaurichthys zoster

The body is generally oval, tall, and compressed. The dorsal profile of the head is quite inclined. The snout is short and pointed. The mouth is terminal, horizontal, and the minute teeth are arranged in four to seven rows. The dorsal and the anal fins are rounded toward the rear. The first seven rays of the dorsal fin are increasingly long. The coloration is white at the center and black toward the front and back. These fish feed on plankton and live in the open waters at the edge of the reef. They grow to be fifteen centimeters in length.

POMACANTHIDAE FAMILY

Blue-Faced angelfish
Pomacanthus xanthometopon

The body is tall, oval in shape, and compressed. The mouth is small and terminal. The dorsal and anal fins have a distinctively rounded rear edge. The caudal fin is truncated. The body presents a delicate reticulated pattern. The head is dark blue, and is speckled with orange, but the eyes are edged in yellow. The caudal fin is orange-yellow and edged with dark blue. On the rear section of the dorsal fin, one can see a black spot. This species feeds of sponges and other encrustant organisms. They live along or in pairs. They grow to be as long as forty centimeters .

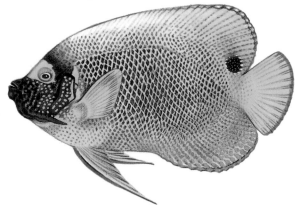

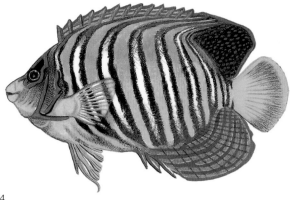

Royal angelfish
Pygoplites diacanthus

The body is less tall than usual in angelfish. The rear edges of the dorsal and anal fins are well developed, but do not exceed the caudal fin. The body has a background coloring of orange yellow, with eight or nine dark blue bands. The eyes are surrounded by two sharply defined dark blue stripes. The dorsal fin has a fairly dark vermiculation, while the anal fin has parallel yellow stripes along the edge of the fin. The young are fairly similar, and have a posterior ocellar spot. This fish grows to a length of thirty centimeters.

Emperor angelfish
Pomacanthus imperator

The shape of the body is nearly oval, with a practically rectilinear forward profile of the head. The snout is very short. The dorsal and anal fins have a rounded forward edge that just exceeds the caudal stalk. The young of this species are dark blue with lighter concentric bands, the last of which forms a closed circle on the caudal stalk. Adults feature many diagonal yellow bands. The eyes are masked by a black stripe edged in light blue, followed by a similar stripe on the operculum. This fish grows to a length of thirty-five centimeters.

ACANTHURIDAE FAMILY

Orangespine unicornfish
Naso lituratus

The body is oval, compressed, and tall toward the front. The head is powerful with a dorsal profile that forms a forty-five degree angle. The snout is pointed; the mouth is small and is lined with sharp teeth with rounded tips. On the sides of the peduncle are two bony plates, each bearing a sharp spine which curves forward. The caudal fin is semilunar, with pointed lobes and long filamentous rays. The coloring is yellowish-brown. The caudal peduncle is orange. Between the eyes is a light yellow spot. The dorsal fin is yellowish-orange, black at the base, with a white edge. This fish attains a length of forty-five centimeters.

Spotted unicornfish
Naso brevirostris

This is the most distinctive of the surgeonfish, easily recognized for its powerful oval body that terminates in a long beak, which in turn extends well beyond the snout. On the sides of the peduncle there are two bony plates which each bear a sharp spine. The caudal fin is rounded. The coloring ranges from greyish-blue to olive brown. The lips are sometimes bluish. The tail features a pale band along the lower edge. This fish has gregarious habits, and attains a length of fifty centimeters.

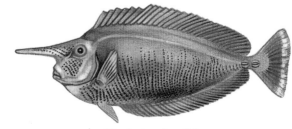

Vlaming's unicornfish
Naso vlammingii

The body is oval, elongated, and compressed. The head has concave dorsal profile. The snout is rounded. The mouth is terminal with protruding lips. The dorsal fin is long, the first rays are filamentous. The ventral fins are small and thoracic. The caudal fin is truncated, with long and filamentous lobes. The coloration is bluish with purple highlights. A dark-blue band distinguishes the eyes and the base of the tail. The coloration can become very light or dark, depending upon the emotional state of the fish. These fish live in schools, and grow to be forty centimeters in length.

Blue surgeonfish
Acanthurus leucosternon

The body is oval and compressed. The snout is short and has a concave profile. The dorsal and anal fins are rounded. The caudal fin is slightly incised. The general coloration of the body is dark blue. The head is black. The dorsal fin is yellow, edged with black and light blue. The caudal fin is light blue at the center, while the edges are black and dark blue. The base of the pectoral fins is orange. There is a yellow spot on the caudal peduncle which indicates the position of the sharp erectile spine. These fish live in schools and are herbivorous; they attain a length of twenty centimeters.

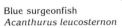

155

Blue-lined surgeonfish
Acanthurus lineatus

The body is elongated and compressed. The snout is rounded. The pectoral fins are sickle-shaped. The caudal fin is lunate, with very elongated lobes. The caudal peduncle has a large spine. The back and upper part of the body are light blue and are adorned with eight or ten yellow striations running lengthwise, edged with black. The belly is light blue, and has orange-yellow highlights. The forward edge of the ventral fins is black. These fish live in relatively large schools in the areas of the reef swept by considerable currents. They grow to be or thirty centimeters in length.

Convict surgeonfish
Acanthurus triostegus

The body is oval and compressed. The dorsal and anal fin are rounded toward the back. The caudal fin is truncated. The spine on the caudal peduncle is short and barely visible. The coloration is silvery-grey with yellow highlights. The dark vertical striations are clearly evident, and the first of these striations masks the eyes. This species is herbivorous and lives in schools in the area around the level parts of the reef. It grows to be as long as twenty to twenty-five centimeters.

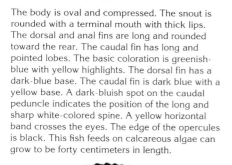

Dussumier's surgeonfish
Acanthurus dussumieri

The body is oval and compressed. The snout is rounded with a terminal mouth with thick lips. The dorsal and anal fins are long and rounded toward the rear. The caudal fin has long and pointed lobes. The basic coloration is greenish-blue with yellow highlights. The dorsal fin has a dark-blue base. The caudal fin is dark blue with a yellow base. A dark-bluish spot on the caudal peduncle indicates the position of the long and sharp white-colored spine. A yellow horizontal band crosses the eyes. The edge of the opercules is black. This fish feeds on calcareous algae can grow to be forty centimeters in length.

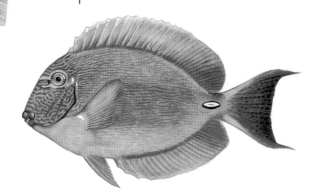

Chocolate Surgeonfish
Acanthurus thompsoni

The body is oblong and compressed. The head is rounded and the snout is short. The tail is lunate, with long pointed lobes. The read edge of the dorsal and anal fins are pointed. The coloration is uniformly dark, brown or olive. The caudal fin is white or yellow. The pectoral fins are bluish. These fish feed on plankton and live above the outer wall of the reef. They grow to be fifteen to twenty centimeters in length.

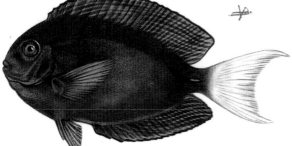

Sailfin tang
Zebrasoma veliferum

The body is compressed, tall, and rounded due to the noteworthy development of the fins. The snout is short, with a protractile terminal mouth. The dorsal fin is well developed and has a typically rounded edge. The anal fin is also quite large. Adults have a basic brownish coloration, with darker bands edged in yellow or orange, continuing along the dorsal and anal fins. The lower half of the flanks is speckled. This species is herbivorous, and attains lengths of thirty-five centimeters.

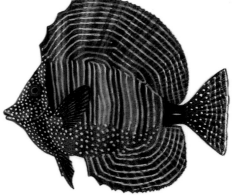

ZANCLIDAE FAMILY

Moorish idol
Zanclus cornutus

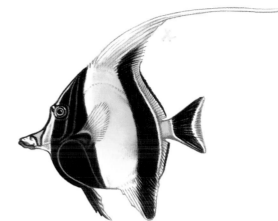

The body is tall, compressed, and disk-shaped. The dorsal profile of the head is rounded, but inclined. The snout is tubular, with a terminal mouth endowed with long teeth. The third ray of the dorsal fin, which is quite elongated, constitutes the most distinctive feature of the species. Near the eye, one can see a very sharp excrescence. The coloration features two broad black strips, separated by a white area, suffused in yellow, extending over the entire dorsal fin. The snout presents a yellow saddle-shaped spot edged in black. The caudal peduncle is yellow. These fish form small schools and are ominvorous; they grow to be twenty-three to twenty-five centimeters in length.

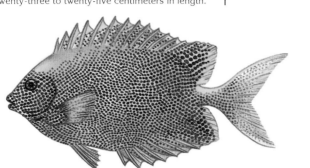

SIGANIDAE FAMILY

Stellate rabbitfish
Siganus stellatus

Oval, compressed body, covered with very small scales. The snout is slightly pointed; the mouth is terminal and is lined with numerous small teeth. The cheeks are covered with large scales. The coloring is generally a greyish-green spangled with small brown spots that tend to become smaller toward the back of the head, where they form a green oval shade at the base of the spines of the dorsal fin. Large black spots are present along the lateral line. This fish grows to a length of forty centimeters.

ELEOTRIDAE FAMILY

Pinkbar shrimb goby
Amblyeleotris aurora

The body is elongated and is more compressed in the rear. The snout is blunt and the eyes are large. There are two dorsal fins. The pectoral fins are well developed and the ventral fins are separated. The basic coloration is quite light, and there are four or five broad pink bands. The tail is yellowish. The lower edge of the mouth is marked by a red striation. This species is territorial, and lives on sandy seabeds where it digs dens that it shares with shrimp. It feeds on worms and small crustaceans. It attains a length of twelve centimeters.

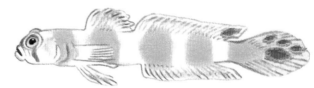

Sixspot Goby
Valenciennea sexguttata

The body is elongated and compressed. The head is blunt. The snout is long, with not very large eyes. The mouth is ample, with well developed anterior canines. The dorsal fins are set very close together. The coloration of the body is light: pinkish-green on the back and pinkish on the belly. Three rows of dark-blue spots extend from the cheeks to the pectoral fin. The fins, in colors ranging from yellow to violet, are spotted or striped. The base of the anal and the caudal fins have orange ocellate spots. These fish live in pairs in dens dug out underneath rocks. They grow to be ten centimeters in length.

Firefish
Nemateleotris magnifica

The body is elongated, rounded toward the front and compressed toward the rear. The snout is short and the eyes are large. The mouth is wide and features a great many teeth, including large canines. There are two dorsal fins: the first has very long erect anterior rays; the second, which is shorter, is symmetrical and opposed to the anal fin. The caudal fin is broad and rounded. The ventral fins are separate. The coloration is light, with yellow highlights on the forward part; red with black-striped fins in the rear part. This species is territorial, and lives in dens dug into the sand, where the fish take shelter when threatened. They grow to be seven centimeters.

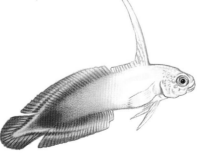

BALISTIDAE FAMILY

Orangestriped triggerfish
Balistapus undulatus

A slightly oval body, tall and compressed, covered with small bony plates. The head is very well developed and measures roughly a third of the length of the body. The eyes are quite far along the side of the fish. The mouth is terminal, and is distinguished by powerful jaws lined with massive teeth. The background coloring is dark, and orange-yellow stripes stand out on it. Bands of the same color surround the mouth. The dorsal and anal fins are light blue. The caudal fin is yellow. This fish grows to a length of seventy centimeters.

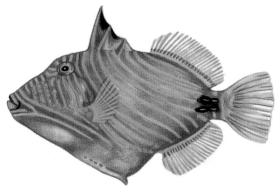

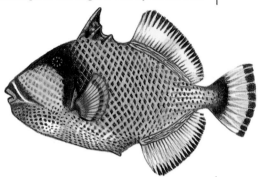

Titan triggerfish
Balistoides viridescens

The shape of the body is typical of the family. The mouth is terminal. There is a deep depression between the eyes. On the stalk of the caudal fin are two to four rows, running lengthwise, of large tubercles. The coloring is greenish; the edges of the fins are black. A black band runs around the upper jaw. The stalk of the caudal fin is fairly light in color. This species is aggressive, especially during the mating season. This fish grows to a length of seventy to seventy-five centimeters.

Boomerang triggerfish
Sufflamen bursa

The body is tall, compressed, and rectangular in shape. The head is conical and the snout is pointed. The mouth is terminal, with thick lips. The incisors protrude. The coloration is light. The head is whitish and the body is suffused with yellow. Between the rear part of the eye and the pectoral fins, one can see two yellow or brownish striations. A narrow white striation runs from the mouth to the anal fin. These fish feed on bottom-dwelling invertebrates, and grow to be twenty centimeters in length.

Redtooth triggerfish
Odonus niger

The body is slightly oval. The head is pointed. The mouth is terminal, and the lower jaw is more developed than the upper. The coloring of the body is blue-black while the head is greenish with blueish stripes leading from the mouth. The caudal fin is semilunar, and the lobes are well developed and quite long. This fish tends to gather in small groups, and grows to a length of fifty centimeters.

Clown Triggerfish
Balistoides conspicillum

The body is oval and compressed. The snout is pointed. The mouth is terminal with protruding incisors. The caudal fin is rounded. The coloring is very vivid, making it easy to recognize this species, one of the best known in its family. The upper portion of the body is dark and speckled with yellow. The lower portion is adorned with large white spots. The lips are orange-yellow and a yellow band is present beneath the eyes. These fish live along the outer wall of the reef, and grow to be as long as fifty centimeters.

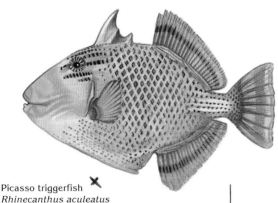

Yellowmargin triggerfish
Pseudobalistes flavimarginatus

This fish has a shape similar to that of P. fuscus, but it is more oval. The teeth are white and arranged in two rows on the upper jaw and only one row on the lower. The background coloring is fairly pale. The forward part of the body, between the snout and the base of the pectoral fins, is pale yellow. The sides are distinguished by numerous small black spots. The edges of the dorsal, anal, and caudal fins are yellowish. This fish grows to a length of sixty centimeters.

Picasso triggerfish ✘
Rhinecanthus aculeatus

The body is oval and compressed. The head is conical, the snout is long and pointed. The forward and ventral part of the body is light in color; the rear part is dark. The mouth is edged with light-blue and yellow, and a striation of the same color extends as far as the pectoral fins. A black band edged with light blue extends from what would be the nape of the neck to the eyes. A series of light-colored oblique bands extend over the flanks. The caudal peduncle has three rows of small black spines. These fish grow to be thirty centimeters in length.

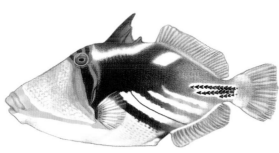

MONACANTHIDAE FAMILY

Harlequin pilefish
Oxymonacanthus longirostris

The body is oval, spindle-shaped, and compressed. The snout is elongated with a terminal mouth that is small but has large lips. The first dorsal fin has a long spinous ray. The coloration is bluish-green, with orange spots that merge in some cases. The mouth is orange. The caudal fin presents a black spot. This fish feeds on coral polyps. It grows to a length of ten centimeters.

TETRADONTIDAE FAMILY

Blackspotted pufferfish ✘
Arothron stellatus

The body is elongated and globular, with an oval silhouette, and is covered with small spines. The young of the species have a rubbery texture, while adults are more flaccid. The mouth is powerful and equipped with two large adjacent dental plates on each jaw. The coloring is typically mottled. In the young, the belly is marked by pronounced black stripes. The base of the pectoral fins is black. This fish propels itself along with its dorsal and anal fins. It is common to encounter this species on the sandy bottoms of lagoons. It grows to a length of 100-120 centimeters.

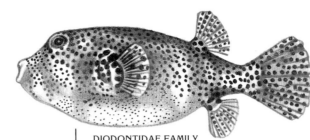

DIODONTIDAE FAMILY

Bleeker's porcupinefish ✳
Diodon liturosus

The body is massive, resembling a large box with rounded corners. The head is small and the eyes are large. The teeth are joined together to form two plaques. The pectoral fins are well developed. The dorsal fin is set posterior to and opposite the anal fin, the caudal fin is small. The brownish-yellow coloration features evident dark splotches edged with white on the back, the eyes, and the flanks. When frightened this fish inflates itself by swallowing water and erecting its spines. These fish grow to be sixty centimeters in length.

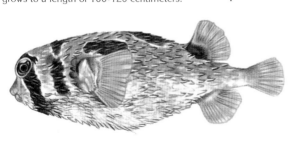

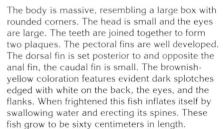

A branch of pink alcyonarian rises above a large coral formation.

Cover

A closely-packed school of snapper crosses a stretch of sea near Ari Atoll.
© Kurt Amsler

*Top left
A group of rays amicably swims around a scuba diver in the waters of North Malé.*
© Kurt Amsler

Back cover

Top Elegant Platax teira circle just under the surface.
© Kurt Amsler

Center A royal angel fish (Pygoplites diacanthus).
Drawing by Monica Falcone/ Archivio White Star

Bottom The illustration reconstructs the typical route of a dive at Embudhu Kandu, on South Malé.
Drawing by Arabella Lazzarin/ Archivio White Star

All the photographs in this book are by Kurt Amsler, except for the following:

Claudio Cangini: pages 40 A, 45 H, 56, 77 G, 84 A-C, 90 A, 94 A-B-C, 95 F, 102 A-B-C-D, 103 E-F, 106 A, 107 E, 100 A-B, 111 E, 114 A-B-D, 120 C, 122 C, 124 B, 129 E, 131 E, 132 C-D, 133 G.

Claudio Gaggioli: page 120 D.

Illustrations of the Dives by Arabella Lazzarin/Archivio White Star

Illustrations of the Fish by Monica Falcone/Archivio White Star